A SPACE FOR BELIEF

Stephen R. White

A Space for Belief

THE PLACE OF THEOLOGY IN FAITH

the columba press

First published in 2006 by
the columba press
55A Spruce Avenue, Stillorgan Industrial Park,
Blackrock, Co Dublin

Cover by Bill Bolger
Origination by The Columba Press
Printed in Ireland by ColourBooks Ltd, Dublin

ISBN 1 85607 521 4

Table of Contents

Introduction

Books about theological topics are rife – works of christology, Trinitarian theology, theodicy, pneumatic theology, systematic theology. Many of them, indeed, are scholarly, profound and illuminating with regard to one aspect or another of theology or with reference to the ways in which certain key concepts are inter-related. What such works tend to have in common, however, is that they are concerned with specific theological arguments and take somewhat on trust – or assume by default – the supreme importance of theological thought in the framework of Christian belief and practice. It is highly questionable, however, whether such an assumption is any longer tenable in the world of the twenty-first century, and indeed it is significant that the majority of theological studies have little impact outside the world of the professionally committed – the world, in other words, of fellow theological scholars, largely in the fields either of systematic theology or philosophical theology.

This is so principally for one of two reasons, either the nature of the subject matter or the manner of its expression. The abstruseness and irrelevance of at least some theological discussion is beautifully illustrated by John Macquarrie in his recent study of Christian mysticism:

> Some years ago I had occasion to write a few paragraphs on Maximus [Confessor] in the course of a book on christology, and while I found some things to admire in his treatment of that subject, I criticised his involvement in the dispute between monothelites and dyothelites. I am still of the opinion that this was an utterly speculative and artificial question, not capable of receiving a rational answer. Those who do at-

tempt to answer the question are guilty of attempting a kind of spiritual anatomy of Christ, in an academic exercise which shows theology at its most irrelevant, both in relation to religion and to serious scholarship.[1]

Similarly, one can readily sympathise with P. D. James' frustration at the way in which all too much theology is done:

> Between lectures [at a theological conference] I looked at some of the theological books on sale in the hall. Most seemed to me totally incomprehensible. Obviously doctrinally and philosophically they would be well above my understanding, but it seemed that the sentences themselves were incomprehensible, a string of polysyllabic words strung together from which I could get no meaning. Theology like other professions has its own obscurantism. The problem is surely that theology should impinge on the lives of ordinary non-theologians if it is to have influence. Surely it can sometimes be written in language the intelligent lay man or woman can understand.[2]

If Macquarrie and James are right, as I believe they are, then the result is that for the vast majority of believers, the world of theology is abstruse and rarefied in the extreme, and there appears no necessity for the 'man in the pew' to become involved in the niceties of christological or trinitarian debate – especially when most of the arguments and illustrations are drawn from the vanished world of Graeco-Roman philosophy.

The most obvious consequence of this is that there is a gulf between professional theologians and 'ordinary believers' which it often seems is virtually impossible to bridge, and this in turn has the potentially disastrous consequence of making most theological thinking seem irrelevant to the everyday practicalities of Christian worship and living. As Kenneth Kearon cogently remarks in his essay 'Ethics, Communities and the Future':

> The development of theological colleges since the late nineteenth century, and more recently the opening of university departments of theology or religious studies has progressed

these disciplines to the extent that they are now on a par with any other third level discipline. This has been at the price of creating a gap which is fast becoming a gulf between theologians and biblical scholars and church members, the elements of whose faith the former claim to be studying. The result is the apparent irrelevance of the one to the other.[3]

The problems to which this apparent irrelevance gives rise will be addressed more fully in the succeeding chapters, but for the present it is enough to suggest that what is needed is not simply more theology, but a new understanding of what exactly theology is, and even more importantly what it can be said to be for. It would appear – not perhaps surprisingly – that for those who are professionally involved, systematic and/or philosophical theology are the *sine qua non* of the Christian life. This may be a thoroughly respectable position in keeping with the voice of tradition, but equally important is the question of its tenability and practical application in the lives of believers – for whose benefit all theology is, in theory, practised. The need for this reforging of the links between theological thinking and the actual lives of believers was brought home to me at the joint Society for the Study of Theology and Irish Theological Association conference in Dublin in March 2005. During the course of a paper which I delivered I quoted a remark by Stanley Hauerwas which encapsulates the depth and immediacy of this relationship: 'Any theology that threatens to become a position more determinative than the Christian practice of prayer betrays its subject. At best, theology is but a series of reminders to help Christians pray faithfully.'[4] At the end of the paper one of the professional theologians present remarked somewhat acidly that she considered that I had overlooked the primary 'constituency' to which theology belonged, that is, the academic one, and she plainly found it either insulting or demeaning to be told that theology was done essentially in the service of faith!

Traditionally theology has established what it is necessary to believe, and defined the bounds of the church community. Thus during the patristic era there occurred the classic controversies

of christological and trinitarian theology as theologians endeav-
oured to give shape and form to their convictions about the
nature of God and his activity in the world. During the course of
these early centuries, and arising out of these controversies, one
can sense a process of gradual petrification at work. Initially
their theology was, presumably, derived at least in part from
Christian experience, and represented an extrapolation into logical terms of the reality which undergirded that experience. This
allowed naturally for a good deal of latitude of interpretation
with regard to the precise details of any particular doctrine, and
for the possibility of genuine doctrinal evolution as new categories of thought or concepts became available or were adopted
by theologians. Thus, for example, the very distinctive *logos*
theology of Justin Martyr, though it continued to exert an influence in succeeding years, became largely superseded, but was
never entirely repudiated or anathematised as the more sophis-
ticated categories of Greek metaphysics began to take over, and
similarly, theologians were frequently content to accept differences of emphasis within a broadly agreed framework of belief.

Gradually, however, the boundaries of this framework became narrower, largely as a result of the series of controversies
(often resolved by the decisions of a council) alluded to earlier.
Increasingly often when significant questions of interpretation
arose, differences of opinion were found to be unacceptable. In
part this reflected the gravity of the questions themselves, and a
sense that there only ever could be one correct answer: after all,
everyone felt, God either was or was not like this or that, and the
theologian's duty was to establish which option was the true
one. At the same time, though, it also stemmed from a growing
rigidity of attitude, as the more closely christology or the Trinity
came to be defined, the more difficult it became to tolerate any
substantial difference of opinion. So, for example, once the supposed excesses of Arianism and Apollinarianism had been ruled
out (and we should always remember, as John Macquarrie reminds us in the context of Cyril and Nestorius, that history has a
habit of being unfair to the ultimate losers of these various de-

bates[5]), there was, as a result of the hardening of attitudes which controversy had engendered, very little room indeed left for manoeuvre. What must be believed about the person of Christ was now established, and was thenceforward merely refined and indeed defined ever more closely by succeeding councils, and dissent represented not creative questioning or discussion, but heresy.

A similar process might be traced in any of the other areas of controversy also, such as that between Augustine and Pelagius over the relationship between human nature, free will and divine grace. In each of these spheres – and thus in the theological realm as a whole – one particular theological viewpoint came to occupy a dominant position. From being initially a creative and logical reflection upon experience and revelation and tradition, theology became itself the governing factor in Christian belief. As Richard Giles delightfully expresses it:

> The great fifth-century battle between the rigid, unyielding dogmatism of Augustine and the experiential, common sense approach of Pelagius resulted in a predictable victory for Goliath, and the church has had to try ever since to live with Augustine's 'savage affirmation of predestination' and his preoccupation with the worthlessness of humankind. The Pelagian concept of human partnership with God and the vital role of free choice have been tut-tutted against ever since … we tend to remain uneasy about Pelagius' confinement in the sin-bin, while Augustine's obsessions continue to ricochet around the church unchallenged.[6]

The tables were thoroughly turned – and experience, revelation, worship, (and indeed anything else) was only acceptable if it was exercised within the limits of belief which the theological establishment itself now prescribed. Theology was no longer merely a servant within the household of faith: it had become the master of the household.

The supremacy thus accorded to specific theological positions (over and above any of the less aggrandising and unfortu-

nately more perishable Christian virtues such as *koinonia* or *caritas*)
has had substantial and lasting consequences for the history and
well-being of the church. Indeed a strong case could be made for
the view that it has been largely responsible for most of the mistrust, divisions and consequent bitterness which have bedev-
illed and all too often disgraced that history. In this context it is
instructive to examine briefly three entirely separate episodes,
spanning a period of some nine hundred years, and to note the
underlying similarity of the inflexible theological positions
which characterise all of these apparently very different and unrelated passages of history.

The first of these episodes is the east/west controversy centred on the year 1054. It would be naïve to pretend that so complex and far-reaching an event as this could be ascribed to any
one single cause, and this beginning of the decisive break between
east and west undoubtedly sprang from a wide variety of factors
each contributing its own momentum to the deterioration of relationships – historic jealousies, rivalry between sees, mistrust of
Rome and individual squabbles to name but a few. Among this
plethora of disputes, however, must also be accounted the
famous – or perhaps infamous – *et filioque* clause asserting the
double procession of the Holy Spirit from the Father and from
the Son, inserted into the creed by the western church following
the traditional emphasis of Augustine and his theological suc-
cessors. Just how important this may have been in provoking
schism may be open to interpretation, but what is certain is that
it has been the occasion of more resentment and continuing bitterness between east and west than almost any other facet of the
conflict. It is an ironic testimony to the power of theology that
two words, hinging on what is after all a relatively minor point
in the context of the whole scope of our understanding of faith,
should have changed the world at once so radically and so de-
structively. Furthermore it is easy to see how such theological
inflexibility can be apparently (though also spuriously) justified.
For in one sense the theologians were right: presumably the
Holy Spirit either does or does not proceed from the Son as well

as from the Father, (although even this assumes that the meta-physical presumptions which undergird the whole schema are more or less accurate in the first place!) and the argument was simply about which of these viewpoints was absolutely and objectively right. However, what got lost (and has remained lost ever since) is the acknowledgement that we are dealing with things which are beyond human certainty, and in the discussion of which a little humility may occasionally not come amiss.

Thus I may wish to opt for single procession to emphasise the unity of the Trinity or to subscribe to double procession to give substance to the relationships within the Trinity, but either way it would hardly be out of place to acknowledge that I could be wrong, and indeed that we are both only using inadequate models, and that therefore your alternative viewpoint may (although it is in one sense irreconcilable with mine) be held with equal integrity. This acknowledgement allows that although we may differ on a matter of some theological moment, nonetheless there is no reason why we should not respect each other's viewpoint, and likewise no reason why we must part company on the issue. Such tolerance was (and still usually is) not acceptable in the debate, and east and west have gone their separate ways for over nine hundred years as a result. The procession of the Holy Spirit has, to date at least, roundly defeated the fellowship of the Holy Spirit.

A recognisably similar picture emerges if we move to the events of the Reformation. Again, it would not be accurate to claim that the Reformation was engendered by primarily strictly theological concerns. Indeed, initially Luther was more motivated by a desire to correct what was amiss in the practice of the church than by any wish to redefine its theological positions. It was not long, though, before theological matters more or less hijacked the reformers' agenda, and again it is easy enough to see why this should have come about. It was natural that in the ecclesiological ferment which the first stirrings of the Reformation sparked off, the new young churches should wish to develop some sort of distinctive identity. They had, according to their perspective, more or less been forced into existence (by the simple

process of excommunication from Rome) and it was understandable that they should wish then to provide a coherent
rationale for their existence – and what better place to look for
such a rationale than in the realm of theology? In each of the new
churches distinctive positions and emphases quickly came to be
established, and it was not long before they were arguing
among themselves as well as with Rome – the divisions concerning baptismal practice and the acceptable limits of what counted
as *adiaphora* being two of the more celebrated.

Thirdly, and turning to the modern era, it can be seen that
little has changed in the academic and professional theological
world, although equally there now appears to be a significant
counter-reaction in the approach of ordinary Christian believers
to the supposed supremacy of theology over practice, indicating, as suggested above, the perceived irrelevance of theology to
the more everyday (and arguably more vital) concerns of
Christian practice and fellowship.

The deliberations, then, of many of the inter-church councils,
most notably ARCIC I and ARCIC II have been inconclusive.
Steps have undoubtedly been made, and there have been landmarks such as the 'Lima Document' and the formal recognition
of one another's baptisms as valid, as evinced by the production
of a 'Joint Baptismal Certificate' endorsed by virtually all of the
main-line churches. In the case of the Anglican-Roman Catholic
dialogue, though, such steps, however much heralded they may
be, represent at best very slender gains and no great departure
from the traditional Roman Catholic position. After all, as far as
baptism is concerned, the Roman Catholic Church has always
acknowledged the validity of lay baptism, and therefore to
allow the validity of baptism within any other communion involves not the recognition of the orders of that communion but
simply the 'emergency' status of that baptism – and when there
is no priest and no likelihood of one the condition of emergency
remains, by definition, in force from birth to death. This may appear an unduly cynical position, but it is one which is entirely
consonant with the facts – which involve, for example, the con-

tinuing formal disavowal of the validity of Anglican orders, a disavowal which, in spite of all the polite words, is still firmly in place.

The central sticking point is, of course, the understanding of, and the supposed validity of the eucharist as it is celebrated in the various communions, and here the Anglican-Roman Catholic dialogues have reached what appears to be an impasse. Intercommunion is perceived by all to be desirable – and as far as Anglicanism is concerned it is entirely possible, the Anglican position being that anyone who is of communicant status within their own denomination is welcome to receive Holy Communion in the Anglican Church. However, it is not as simple as this, and for Roman Catholicism intercommunion involves such things as the validity of Anglican orders, not at present acknowledged, and therefore it must, of necessity, depend upon the resolution of the underlying theological and doctrinal controversies. It must follow, not precede, theological agreement (an agreement which it must be said looks to be one dictated by Rome). This agreement has not been, and is not currently forthcoming, and therefore in theory intercommunion is not possible. Indeed, the traditional hedges and boundaries have been in large measure reinforced by the publication by the Roman Catholic bishops of *One Bread, One Body*, and by the encyclical *Dominus Iesus* which appeared on 6 August 2000 and declared that the various reformed churches were 'ecclesial communities' and not churches in the 'proper sense'.

Here, though, lies the crucial flaw in the argument, and the potential irrelevance of theological nit-picking. For intercommunion patently is possible and is happening regardless of the decisions of the curia, ARCIC theologians and the Roman hierarchy. I am writing from a situation in Ireland (with a more traditionally minded Roman Catholic Church than many other countries) and yet I have witnessed a number of Roman Catholic Parish Priests and members of their congregations receiving Holy Communion in the Church of Ireland (most notably in recent times the decision of the Irish President Mary McAleese to receive Holy Communion in Christ Church Cathedral, Dublin) and inviting the Church of Ireland congregation to do the same on certain occasions. The theologians may argue that theological unity is a pre-condition of intercommunion, but for local congregations the reality is the exact reverse, and one day theology will have to catch up with the present facts of Christian practice, in which the desire for fellowship has overcome the academic demands of theological purity.

This brief excursus into the history of theology and its supremacy, and the relatively recent counter-reaction to it, explain the immediacy and urgency of the need for a reappraisal of the status of theology. Quite simply it has got itself into something of a dead end. It has lost the spirit which gives life and become the letter which kills, and this has happened because theology has ousted Christian experience, prayer, worship and practice from their place and has become itself (or attempted to become) the governing framework for these other things. It is the contention of this study, therefore, that what is needed is that theology should, as it were, take a step back and become an entity of the second order rather than of the first.

This volume is concerned with exploring why this step is necessary and outlining how it is to be taken, but it is evident that this reappraisal of the function of theology will have further consequences, both intellectually in that it opens up a new space for the idea of a Christian unknowing, and ecclesiologically in that it heralds a move away from the traditional concept of the church as an 'ark of salvation' which provides all the answers, and towards a vision of the church as a people *in via* and perpetually seeking ever more of the truth. It is my intention to explore these two areas more fully in two further volumes to be entitled *A Space for Unknowing: The Place of Agnosis in Faith* and *A Space for All: The Seeking Church*. At this stage, however, it is sufficient to note that this reappraisal of the function of theology will require much courage of the church (and especially of those with a professional and personal interest in the subject) because it appears to be a step which undermines the place and importance of theology in the Christian scheme. On the contrary, however, I believe that it is a step which allows theology to fulfil its true role which is to undergird and make sense of the rich variety of Christian experience and practice, rather than, as at present, to overshadow this experience and practice and threaten to obscure or even to deaden them. It is a step which would at once benefit the church's life and also rescue the study of theology from its present somewhat invidious position – a position which we must now turn to consider in more depth.

CHAPTER ONE

A Discipline under Threat

Initially it may seem absurd to suggest that theology, and in particular systematic theology, is a discipline under threat. On the contrary, it may be argued, the theology 'industry' is apparently alive and well. New books and articles continue to appear, and the flow of doctoral and masters theses remains unchecked. Where, it may reasonably be asked, is the problem?

The mere fact that something continues to exist and seems, indeed, even to flourish is, though, no guarantee of its underlying vitality and health. It is quite possible for the central purpose to have departed from an organisation or even an organism and for the outer shell merely to continue to exist in a somewhat aimless fashion. It is a little like a charitable trust, the reason for whose original existence has disappeared, but whose trustees continue to meet in order to decide how to re-invest the funds for which no-one any longer has any use. Technically the trust certainly continues to exist, and indeed, with no-one to call on them, has ever-increasing funds at its disposal, but it cannot be reasonably claimed that this existence any longer has a great deal of purpose to it. And one day the penny will drop, and the trust will be, as it should have been long ago, wound up.

It may be presumptuous or even shocking for one who stands outside the ranks of professional scholars to say so, but from the perspective of parish and diocesan life this is, broadly, what appears to have happened to the academic study of theology – that it has lost its underlying purpose and exists in a vacuum as an interesting academic pastime (which is itself not infrequently hi-jacked by philosophy) of little immediate value to the pressing needs of the church. Indeed, precisely this problem is noted by Marc Ouellet in his perceptive study of Balthasar's determination to keep theology focused on its essential nature. In his theology Balthasar has been attempting, says Ouellet, to counteract 'one of the major problems of modern theology' which he describes as being 'the divorce between theology and spirituality'.[1]

To say that theology has lost its way in this manner begs the question of what theology is *for* – not so much what it is in itself, but what is its purpose and why does it matter that theological concepts should be thought out in a disciplined way? To this question there are probably as many answers as there are questioners, and what follows is therefore necessarily a personal assessment of the role of theology in the church's life. It may be one which differs from, or goes further than the opinions of some professional academic theologians, but it is one which, I believe, manages meaningfully to relate the academic study of theology to the day-to-day needs of dioceses, parishes and individual believers.

The business of theology, then, is, I suggest, to attempt to do four things, all of which stand in a natural and progressive relationship with one another. The first two are concerned more largely with the question of what theology does, and the second two approach the issue of what it is for – why its contribution to the life of the church is potentially so vital. First, the study of theology seeks to provide a rational statement of what we believe and why we believe it. Clearly this task will depend in part upon the work of other scholars in related disciplines, both biblical and historical, but the distinctive input of the scholar of systematic theology is to give shape and form and, vitally, a contemporary voice to the necessarily more fragmentary productions of these other disciplines, and to ensure that, as far as is humanly possible, Christian belief is internally coherent and free from self-contradiction.

This leads naturally to the second aspect of the theological task, which is to relate the different parts of Christian belief as cogently and compellingly as possible and, in turn, to relate this complex of belief to the findings of other disciplines and to our understanding and experience of the world.

Thus far there is nothing startling or unorthodox about these suggestions as to the function of theology. Indeed some such similar sort of understanding would be found in many an introduction or preface to works on systematic theological topics, such as the extremely lucid and forthright statement made by John Macquarrie right at the beginning of his renowned *Principles of Christian Theology*:

> Christian theology seeks to think the church's faith as a coherent whole. It aims not only at showing the internal coherence of the Christian faith, that is to say, how the several doctrines constitute a unity, but also at exhibiting the coherence of this faith with the many other beliefs and attitudes to which we are committed in the modern world. Only if these tasks are accomplished can the faith be held intelligently and be integrated with the whole range of human life.[2]

Later in the same Preface, however, Macquarrie himself goes further and acknowledges (though only in passing) the existence of a vital link between theology and what he calls 'Christian action', and it is this link which I would argue has all too often not been made, and on the recognition of which link the third and fourth elements in the task of theology depend.

Thirdly, then – and arising out of the two elements so far discussed – theology exists to provide a framework of belief and understanding within which the Christian faith can be practised, both in terms of our calling to worship and prayer and in terms of daily Christian living. It should be noted that I have referred to a 'framework' of belief rather than to a strait-jacket of belief, and this framework needs to be flexible and responsive to the changing needs and understanding of the church. Christian theology creates what I would wish to call a 'space for belief', rather than to chain that belief down too closely at every point or to pre-determine on *a priori* grounds the limits of God's activity or of our own experience of him. That this is and must be the nature of theology is clearly acknowledged by John Austin Baker in his exploration of *The Faith of a Christian*:

In reality it is doubtful whether any Christian, however devout, actually believes only and always what the community of faith decrees. For one thing, how many Christians actually know and understand with complete accuracy and in full detail what their community does decree? For another, there are nearly always some areas in the mind of any member where she or he guards the right to at least a private agnosticism. Both these positions are perfectly compatible with loyalty to the organisation and with respect for its teaching authority. But the fundamental fact is that no two people have exactly the same faith. This is inevitable in the nature of the case. It is, after all, the purest orthodoxy to insist that God is ultimately in himself unknowable, a mystery to which our human words point only by analogy, some more accurately than others. So how could we ever expect that any two human beings, all of whom differ in inherited make-up and cultural formation, should have identical understandings of God.[3]

He then further points out that this has consequences for the way in which we do theology, in that we must be 'prepared to replace a good many of the time-honoured set pieces with new versions.'[4]

Thus systematic theology in particular needs constantly to be aware that it is working always with pictures and models which will inevitably and invariably be less than adequate representations of the reality which they depict, and it needs to allow for the fact that these pictures and models may need to evolve or change from time to time in order more accurately to reflect the state of our understanding of that reality. Furthermore, there is a very real sense in which the function of theology is to endeavour to mark out the rational bounds of Christian belief rather than to delineate that belief too closely at every point, and thus there needs to be an acceptance of the fact that a creative diversity of opinion is not only possible, but even desirable.

Thus, for example, if we are endeavouring to formulate a series of statements about the attributes of God, there is only so much that can be said. We need to bear in mind Martin Henry's remark that the most important statement we can make about God – more important than discussing any of his attributes – is that 'God is'.[5] And when we come to use more language than this about God we need equally to bear in mind all of its short-comings, and those of our own understanding:

> Descriptions of the use of language to refer to God as metaphorical or analogical are not to be regarded as ways of naming precise and well-defined methods of application; they are rather variant forms of reminder that the language being used is to be understood only in some very indirect and oblique manner. All language about God incorporates an apophatic as well as a cataphatic aspect. Whatever positive language is affirmed, has also to be denied, at least to the extent of acknowledging that we do not fully understand how it applies.[6]

Thus theology can realistically only affirm the general appropriateness of some qualities and deny the appropriateness of others. What it can not do is to pretend to pin down exactly what these attributes may mean as far as the nature of God in himself is concerned. That is, we may postulate that God has the attribute of goodness or of truth, but we cannot define with any clarity exactly what this looks like when applied to God or what its limits may be. We are, inevitably, limited by our own human perceptions, and in the end we can only view the attributes of God in human terms and try creatively to imagine what they might mean in divine terms – and at the same time we must always recognise that this is what we are doing, and therefore we must also avoid claiming any final objective certainty for our necessarily speculative formulations. Similarly, too, we should as a result of this, realise that we cannot, from our 'knowledge' of his attributes, make any too concrete predictions as to how God should, will or must act. If theology creates a 'space for belief' from the human perspective, it must leave a space for God also – a space in which he is acknowledged to be ultimately beyond our human formulations of him and is understood to be in no way constrained by such formulations.

The fourth and final element of the task of theology again springs from all that has been said thus far. This element is, in a sense, the 'practical' application of doctrine in the day to day life of the church. For the ultimate function of theology (and indeed its ultimate purpose, as was noted in the quotation from Stanley Haeurwas in the Introduction) is to inform and clarify our understanding of what we do in worship, prayer and daily living, and therefore even to influence the forms of prayer we use or the way in which we approach God – a function and purpose which Balthasar has exemplified in his life-long commitment to 'holy theology', and which Michael Ramsey illustrates with characteristic deftness when he exhorts the church to 'continue to do theology to the sound of church bells'.[7] This may even directly affect the language and vocabulary in which we address God, and it should certainly affect how we think of him and speak of him in relation to the events of our own lives. Two brief illustrations may perhaps best illuminate how this might be so – illustrations which will be enlarged upon in the succeeding chapters as we consider in more detail the role of theology in a variety of aspects of the church's life.

Clearly a central concern of the church, then, is its life of prayer, both as expressed in public worship and in private devotion. There is a real question-mark, though, over how far the kind of language in which we habitually address God truly reflects what we actually think and believe about his nature and activity. It is almost a cliché to say so, but much of our public prayer at least is of the 'shopping list' variety, in which (overtly and verbally and regardless of what we may think we are doing) we appear to be reminding God of things which he might otherwise have overlooked, or specifying how best the deity might obligingly display his benevolence and power by answering our prayers. The words and forms of prayer we use do not match the ways in which we actually think of God. Why this is so will be considered in more detail at a later stage, but for the present it is sufficient to suggest that it should be the business of theology to bridge this gap and ensure that belief and practise do succeed in walking hand in hand.

The failure of theology to become a reality in the lives of believers is even more clearly displayed when it comes to reflecting on how we perceive God as acting or as reacting towards
events in human lives. The daily round of parish routine provides countless examples of God 'calling people home', or 'caus-
ing' this or that illness or death for some purpose of punishment
or in order to 'test the faith' of the afflicted person, and I have an
unpleasant feeling that this genuinely is how many people perceive God as acting and responding. And that is fine if (and only
if) that is indeed how we understand God theologically. If, however, (as I believe) that is not the case, then much of our life is
being lived under the pernicious and debilitating influence of
thoroughly bad theology, and our best understandings have not
yet permeated to the level of everyday parish life, with the result
that many believers are still saying things and ascribing actions
to God which a more enlightened theological approach would
wish utterly to repudiate.

In neither of these two cases of prayer and daily life, then,
does theology at present appear to fulfil the fourth part of the
task which we have outlined; but this is no reason why that task
should be deemed impracticable, or why it should not again be
proclaimed as vital.

Having thus outlined these four central constituents of the
theological task, it should of course be noted that this task is a
never-ending and cyclical one. It is, in a sense, a task which
every generation begins afresh, as Kierkegaard reminds us in
Fear and Trembling.[8] It is not enough for the practitioners of theology to work through the series of elements and then sit back
and congratulate themselves on a job well done. If this happens
then the study of theology is liable quickly to stagnate.
Theology, and with it the Christian faith in its entirety, is only
kept alive if, in turn, our experience of God in worship, prayer
and daily living causes us again and again to return to our formulations and models and to refine or even occasionally to redefine our conception of God and of his activity.

As was acknowledged earlier, this is a personal assessment

of the role and function of theology, and it makes no claim to any kind of privileged status. Some such assessment as this is, however, essential to the well-being both of theology itself and of the church, and it is therefore somewhat disturbing that there is the gulf between theology and Christian practice which we have noted. On the one side of that gulf are the ways in which people actually live and think and speak, and on the other side there is a great deal of theological study which appears to be conducted in an ecclesiastical vacuum and to be relevant and applicable only to its own world and to its own devotees.

To the world outside this academic hot-house, its productions appear, with rare exceptions, as was noted in the Introduction, to be either deadening and devaluing in their attitude towards Christian experience, or simply irrelevant as not being meaningfully connected with that experience. At present this would appear to be so in three major respects, and as a consequence of these it is possible to predict a further dangerous dilemma looming for the future.

To begin with, then, it is more than possible (and I suspect that a substantial percentage of Christians would so regard it) to see the minutiae of theological debate as being somewhat arid when compared with the richness of their own experience of God. This, perhaps, would not matter if theology did not make some sort of regulative claims *vis-à-vis* that experience and its interpretation. But it does make just such claims in that it lays down the structure of belief, and therefore, by implication threatens, at least, to pre-judge the validity of experience according to that imposed pattern of belief. This is in no sense a new problem. It has arisen whenever an individual or a group has found that their experience (to them overwhelming) has been invalidated by the theological 'thought-police' of the 'establishment'. Radicals such as Francis of Assisi, and the genuinely unorthodox but devout such as Margery Kempe have all faced this problem and had to endure such a confrontation.

Clearly in comparing the claims of theology and experience it would be easy to be simplistic and indeed naïve, and to appear to suggest that experience is the sole governing factor. Obviously this would be disastrous for any kind of structured belief, as it would lead to a doctrineless 'anything goes' situation and therefore to the rapid decline of those beliefs themselves. To insist on the primacy of experience in this way would be to threaten the integrity of the Christian faith, if not, in the long run, to sign the death warrant of its existence in any organised form. What is argued here, however, is not this kind of theological nihilism, but merely the fact that the hold of theology has been (and sometimes still is) too tight and that it seriously deadens that experience of God on which it itself, ultimately, feeds.

Ideally it would be the case that experience should be tempered by exposure to theological reflection, and its insights refined by that reflection, rather than that it should simply be killed off by the inflexibility of any supposedly infallible theological categories. As far as theology itself is concerned, the danger is that if there is a direct confrontation between the two and if people are forced to choose (as with Francis of Assisi and Margery Kempe) then they will (even at their own cost) choose experience, which has the merit of being their own, and being therefore for them very powerful, and theology is then left with the odour of irrelevance surrounding it and very often the task, later even if not at the time, of coming to terms with and catching up with the reality of experience. Theology and experience belong together, and their relationship should be one of mutual informing and reinforcement, but this cannot happen when the categories of theological thought (necessarily primarily intellectual) come to have – or claim to have – a stranglehold over experience with its wealth of spiritual and emotional resonances.

From this rejection of the devaluing and deadening hold of an inflexible theological structure over experience stems the second of the three major issues facing theology at the present time – its frequently perceived irrelevance to the everyday world of Christian living. It is necessary to tread extremely carefully at this point, since my own belief is precisely that theology is vital to this everyday world, and that it is the perception of irrelevance which is the danger – a perception which the study of theology tends to wish upon itself by its olympian aloofness from the cares and concerns of the world.

The problem, perhaps, is similar to that which confronted Caesar's wife – as with her purity, theology must not only possess relevance but be seen to possess it; and if it does not, then its fate is likely to be similar to hers also! In other words, theology, like any other discipline, is quite entitled to be concerned with the finer points of its own debates – indeed it is also legitimate for it to be concerned with its own historical development and to be discussing and evaluating the terms and concepts adopted in past ages – but I believe, however, that it does, at the same time, need to indicate how and why these debates (however intrinsically interesting they may be to those who enjoy them) are relevant to us here and now. If this is not done, and if theology is perceived to be conducted without reference to the present needs of the church – at every level, including that of the humblest parish – then all of this thought, be it ever so profound, is a mere academic exercise; and if this is the perception, then unfortunately all of the thought and insight and all of the traditional terms and categories and all of the ideas associated with them will be consigned to the dump of the past. For the sake of its own survival (and, in fairness to theology, for the sake of the church and its life also) theology has got to show why it matters (and matters desperately) why such-and-such a view is appropriate today – how we arrive at it, and how it coheres with all of the other things which we believe and experience, and why it makes sense of who God is and how he/she acts here and now. If it does not succeed in doing this, then it is – rightly, and however clever it may be in itself – ultimately and fatally irrelevant.

The notion of relevance is also closely bound up with the third of the issues confronting theology. This is its position with regard to some of the huge and urgent challenges which face Christians today, both individually and corporately in certain parts of the world. Many of us are fortunate enough not to be personally involved in major religious or political controversy, and we can therefore ignore (or not even realise to begin with) the demands which such controversy may place upon our understanding of Christian theology. For others, though, including those in all of the Irish churches, there is a pressing need to find some sort of new and constructive way to relate belief and experience in order to achieve reconciliation and fresh understanding between different outlooks. Admittedly here in Ireland the situation is by no means entirely religious, and it is very hard to separate out the varied strands of religion, politics, nationality and so on. At whatever level, however, there is a religious dimension to the situation, and hitherto theological reflection has not significantly contributed towards understanding and reconciliation and may even, by its inflexibility, have been said to have militated against such harmony.

It is all very well to offer these general comments, but what do they mean in more specific terms? By way of answer it may be suggested that whilst theology is not obviously at the heart of the complex politico-religious distinctions and even divisions in Ireland, it does nonetheless have a potentially substantial bearing on it. For one strand in the situation is that there are significant differences of theological opinion (and strictly of doctrine) between Roman Catholic and non-Roman Catholic understandings of faith – as there are also between Presbyterian and Church of Ireland understandings and so on – and these have become magnified in the Irish context, and on each side (or at least among the more extreme elements on each side) the conviction of unalterable and complete 'rightness' has taken root and has indeed been sedulously nurtured. Thus Roman Catholics know they are 'right' in affirming their devotion to Mary, the primacy of the Pope, the sacrifice of the Mass and so on. Equally, however, the various Protestant denominations 'know' that the Roman Catholics are 'wrong' in so affirming. Just as we noted was the case with the controversies of earlier centuries, theology has attempted to decide between two options and proclaim the rightness of the one and the wrongness of the other. The problem here, though, is that each option has been defined in opposite

ways by the differing parties, and the result is a further hardening of positions and an ever greater inflexibility in religious matters, which in turn has fed into the all too frequent political in-
transigence of all parties.

That said, the question remains: what positive contribution
might a new appraisal of theology make to this situation? The
answer to this question hinges, I believe, on the understanding
of theology outlined briefly above as delineating a 'space for belief' within which there is room for creative discussion and difference of opinion. At present there is no such space, and the dis-
puted points are necessarily right or wrong – and if the game
continues to be played according to the current rules it is extremely hard to see a way out of this impasse. However, if the
rules were to be relaxed even slightly and the place of human
imagination and creative intuition were to be more fully acknowledged, then perhaps the inflexibility might disappear
once the shackles of supposed objective certainty had been set
aside, and the terms 'right' and 'wrong' might be replaced by
the more elastic and less pejorative notion of 'difference'. This
would in no way be to make our theology (or rather theologies)
so diffuse as to be meaningless, since there is already room in
the household of faith for these various differences of opinion.
To enlarge the boundaries in this way would merely enable the
members of that household to move more freely from room to
room rather than being, at they are at present, under the same
roof but confined to their own quarters.

I have chosen to use the Irish context as an illustration simply
because it is the one with which I am most familiar, but the same
need for theology to find a new relevance in the face of great issues would, presumably, apply in many other instances also – a
church needing to rebuild both itself and a nation in Rwanda
and to heal grievous wounds; and a church striving valiantly to
continue the process of racial healing in South Africa, to name
but two further possible instances, to say nothing of the church's
response to the international issues of war, justice and HIV/
AIDS. What appears certain is that theology cannot simply take

its own relevance to the life of the church on trust, but must, if it is genuinely to flourish and be of service to the church, discover and re-assert its own relevance to whatever events, crises or challenges may be facing the church in any age – our own not excepted.

It is true that certain varieties of theology have succeeded in achieving this relevance and have proved themselves to be of great service to Christians in many situations, and one might think especially of theologies such as feminist theology, woman-ist theology and liberation theology in this context. Two points need to be made in this connection, however. First, that these theologies are only partial, and the same relevance and service needs to be achieved by theology as a whole, rather than just particular theologies addressed to specific sections of the com-munity or geographical locations. Secondly, in case it should be thought that unchecked radicalism of the kind which charac-terised the early productions of liberation theology, for example, is being advocated here, it should be remembered that all theol-ogy is done in the context of the wider church and not in isol-ation. This provides some safeguards, in that any excesses which flourish in one context may well be refined and purged through contact with other theologies from that wider church community. That this is so is borne out by the experience of liberation theo-logy itself, whose central theses have been understood and broadly accepted by many, but some of whose unacceptable conclusions have been challenged by others, and whose ideas have been refined over time by a process of mutual interplay and synthesis between differing perceptions.

Having suggested that in these three ways doctrine is often perceived as either stultifying or irrelevant, it is instructive to note that the current state of theological scholarship would ap-pear to be itself a symptom of this perception, and that the ap-parent health of theological studies is merely that – an appear-ance and not a reality. For any discipline to remain vital and healthy, one generation of thinkers and scholars must succeed another: no generation can afford to rest upon the laurels of the previous one. At the present, however, this succession of talent would not appear to be in evidence either for systematic theology specifically, or for the realm of theology in general. The reputation of theology as an academic discipline rests largely on the shoulders of a gradually diminishing number of senior figures who are, thankfully, still thinking and writing into their advancing years, but it is somewhat unclear who will succeed these figures in only a few years' time. Where are the 35-45 year old theologians who will become the Moltmanns and Macquarries of the next generation? I would be delighted to be proved wrong on this point, and to have the identity of innumerable such people pointed out to me, but my own perception (and that of at least one reputable theological commentator) is that these figures are not readily identifiable at the present time. And it may be that one reason for this apparent dearth is that the best minds of our generation are not willing to devote themselves to a discipline whose vitality and relevance are at best uncertain. If this is so, then the picture comes to resemble a downward spiral, as what was a symptom of decline becomes itself a cause of a further loss of confidence and life.

To some it will no doubt appear that the foregoing picture of the current state of theology has been painted in unnecessarily sombre tones. Whether this is so, or whether a more cautionary approach such as that outlined here is justified, is something which only the future (and with it theology's own response to that future) will make plain. If the present assessment is erroneous then, presumably, all will continue to be well. If, however, any or all of the above remarks should turn out to be well-founded, then the future health of theology will depend entirely upon its response to the issues we have outlined. Again, if an appropriate response and re-appraisal is forthcoming then a temporary crisis will have been averted. But if theology should prove unequal or resistant to this task of self re-appraisal it will, I suggest, find itself firmly impaled upon the horns of an extremely uncomfortable and potentially disastrous dilemma – and from this point onwards extrication and subsequent revival would prove increasingly difficult.

This dilemma is directly related to the issues of relevance and stultification which we have discussed above, and its essence is the simple question: if theology cannot face the necessary process of self re-appraisal, which of these two almost equally unfortunate alternatives is it destined, in the long run, to embrace? This question will in turn be decided by the 'success' of theology in exerting its authority over the church and the practice of faith.

The first possibility then (if theology fails to assert its authority), is that of ever-increasing irrelevance to the ongoing life of faith of the vast majority of Christian believers. In other words, the present state of affairs is one which in this case will continue and indeed intensify, until theology has become completely divorced from the realities of Christian experience, and the niceties of its positions have entirely ceased to matter to anyone except the few who continue aridly to debate them. Thus, for all its pronouncements, theology would ironically cease to matter to anyone, and the climate might well rapidly become one of anarchy in which 'anything goes' in terms of belief. It would be foolhardy to claim that the present situation is as extreme as this, but we are, potentially, only a relatively few steps away from such a position. For all its potential importance, for example, how many people appear to be genuinely concerned about, and well-versed in the so-called 'new debate about God'. In this debate scholars are contemplating matters which are, in theory, of ultimate importance – but the danger is that this is all it remains: a debate 'in theory' only. If such matters can effectively by-pass (and be allowed by those concerned to continue to by-pass) the attention of the mass of believers, then we would appear to be already well on the way towards a condition of almost total theological irrelevance.

Equally real, and equally damaging, is the second possibility which might ensue if theology, without having adapted and reformed itself, yet manages successfully to assert its authority over the life of the church. If this happens, then the danger is at the diametrically opposite point from that of irrelevance: namely, that theology becomes an aggressive and domineering force in the church's life. A system of theology which is 'successful' in these terms will substantially deaden (or at least enervate) the church's life by restricting the scope of Christian experience and understanding to its own increasingly narrow channels. Theology, in this aggressive mode, will come to dominate all other aspects of the Christian life and become the filter for (and the final arbiter of) everything else. Furthermore, and lest at the present time this should seem a somewhat far-fetched scenario, it should be pointed out that this is precisely what is happening in the more fundamentalist reaches of the church already. Expectations of experience are laid down in advance – God acts in this or that way if we do such-and-such a thing; and even more dangerously, moral positions are taken up and fanatically imposed on the grounds that God is definitely for or against a particular position because we know him (from scripture, and from theology which in these circles slavishly follows scripture) to be this or that kind of a God. Theology – and frequently bad or pernicious theology – has already come in fundamentalist Christianity (and also, by way of comparison, in fundamentalist Islam) to dictate the limits and indeed the precise nature of Christian (or Muslim) experience and attitudes. The bulk of the church has so far escaped this servitude, but it would be rash to disregard the negative potential of theology in this regard for the future of the church – after all, I doubt whether Luther determinedly hammering pieces of paper to a church door in Wittenburg appeared to pose much of a threat to the might of the Roman Catholic Church either.

Enough has been said here to suggest that theology is – and perhaps contrary to appearances – a discipline under threat, and also, importantly, a discipline which carries within itself a threat in return to the health of the wider life of the church. It has become clear, even in the course of this necessarily somewhat cursory examination, that in order to avoid both of these opposing threats, the study of theology must subject itself to a searching process of self re-appraisal. Having outlined something of the general nature of the problems which confront theology at the present time, it is necessary now to turn in more detail to a number of areas of the Christian life and to attempt to indicate at least some of the ways in which theology needs to become more intimately (and more reciprocally) related to them. In this examination the concept of reciprocity will be of fundamental significance, for the relationship between Christian theology and the Christian life must be, if it is to be a wholesome one, symbiotic. For theology can only fulfil its true function and be itself healthy in such a relationship, and likewise every aspect of Christian experience needs the underpinning and coherent rationale of a theological structure if it is to continue to be identified as authentically Christian. It will be the contention of this study that such a creative symbiotic relationship between theology and life is, whilst at present substantially lacking, not only desirable but attainable.

CHAPTER TWO

Theology and Public Worship

Public worship is, and always has been, at the heart of the church's life, and for this reason, if for no other, it is appropriate to make it the starting point for a closer assessment of the relationship of theology to the life of the church. The centrality of public worship to that life is hardly in doubt: symptomatic of this primacy is the fact that the failure to conduct public worship is one of the few offences for which even a freehold clergyman can be deprived of his benefice. More than this though, public worship is the principal time at which the church gathers together to profess its faith, confess its sins, make its intercessions, and celebrate its sacramental union with God. It is a time at which (and an activity in which) the church is most distinctively itself, and in which it is most readily identifiable as the church in the eyes of the world. For all of these reasons, then, it is, presumably, a time and an activity in which 'what the Church believes' is most clearly proclaimed and most open to inspection.

The fundamental question which must be asked, then, is: 'What do we learn or infer about the church's beliefs by attending public worship or by studying its liturgical forms as set out in its various prayer books?' Curiously, the answer to this question varies depending upon which aspects of the church's belief one happens to be referring to. In terms of straightforward confessional statements about who God is, the answer is unexceptionable, in that much worship contains one or another of the historic credal statements of belief. From this it might appear that our theology is faithfully reflected in worship – and so it is in this rather limited sense. However, the answer to our question is very different when one moves from simple credal definition to what one might call 'applied theology' – in other words our understanding of how this God (whom we have just so neatly defined) actually acts, and equally how we understand our relationship with him and interpret our own status as created beings.

In these respects the church's beliefs as stated (or even implied) in worship are substantially more problematical, and the gap between theology and Christian practice (in this case the practice of worship) becomes immediately apparent.

In what follows I shall draw my examples from the Church of Ireland's *Book of Common Prayer* 2004, and I shall do so for two reasons. First, it is the liturgy with which I am most familiar; and secondly, it is, in terms of the language of intercession especially, more 'fixed' than that of any of the other denominations (Roman Catholicism included), since in all of these other denominations there is a greater flexibility to allow for the prayers of the faithful to be formulated in their own words. Clearly it is easier to discuss that which is fixed, but I would argue from my experiences of hearing more '*ad hoc*' intercessions that the attitudes and theological assumptions which underlie them are broadly similar. I use my own tradition merely by way of illustration, but the gist of what follows would, I am certain, apply equally well to most public worship in most denominations.

Some of the more obvious difficulties stem from the innate conservatism of church worship, resulting in the Anglican communion in a continuing, and indeed entirely understandable devotion, to the forms of worship enshrined in the 1662 *Book of Common Prayer* and its various revisions in the different provinces of the Anglican Communion. For all the beauty of its language, though, its use is not without problems in the world of the twenty-first century.

In using these forms of worship, then, we are committing ourselves to conducting our worship in the thought forms – and also, of course, the specific vocabulary and syntax – of four hundred and fifty years ago, (remembering, of course, that much of the material pre-dates the 1662 Prayer Book by over one hundred years), and this, of necessity, creates an instant gap be-

tween our statements of belief and the actual nature of those beliefs themselves as we hold them today. This gap can be overcome, and the old *Book of Common Prayer* can therefore still claim
to be a meaningful form of worship for the present day, but in
order to do this successfully there needs to be a great deal of
thought and careful explanation and translation of meaning in
which these ancient ways of thought are made appropriate and
creative in our own time. In the absence of such translation, the
gap remains and worship and theology remain at odds.

Examples of this problem could be illustrated almost at ran-
dom, but it is sufficient here to cite just two instances, both of
which occur in the regular weekly worship of the church,
whether at Morning and Evening Prayer or in the celebration of
the Holy Communion: that is, the forms which are used for confession and for intercession, forms which, whatever we may say
in the creed, actually reveal most accurately what we appear to
believe about our relationship with God and about his activity
in the world and in human lives.

The forms which we use for confession, though different in
the daily offices and the service of Holy Communion, are
nonetheless both (and in similar fashion) theologically loaded.
Both forms are concerned to stress our innate sinfulness – a sinfulness which borders on utter depravity and spiritual bank-
ruptcy – and to invoke the mercy of a righteously angry and potentially retributive God. At Morning Prayer and Evening Prayer
we declare that, 'there is no health in us', and describe ourselves
as 'miserable offenders', and during the service of Holy
Communion we, 'acknowledge and bewail our manifold sins
and wickedness, Which we, from time to time, most grievously
have committed, By thought, word, and deed, Against thy
Divine Majesty, Provoking most justly thy wrath and indign-
ation against us,' having done which we then proclaim that we
'are heartily sorry for these our misdoings; The remembrance of
them is grievous unto us; The burden of them is intolerable.' The
picture of our condition which this reveals is one which owes
everything to a particular reforming strain of 'salvation' theo-

logy and nothing whatsoever to any kind of 'creation' theology. We are sinners doomed to perish, and only saved from our fate by the overflowing mercy of a God who has every right to punish. There is no goodness inherent in the creation or in humanity – created for wrath we can only supplicate and hope to be redeemed by mercy.

To confess one's sins in this way might have seemed entirely appropriate in 1549 (or even in 1662) when the words which were spoken did indeed faithfully reflect the prevailing theological understanding among the reformed churches, but this is, for most of us, no longer the situation today. Ideas about the atonement have been modified, and from a wide variety of sources (including 'environmental theology') new attention has been focused on the intrinsic value and goodness of the creation and of human life, an attention which has altered our perception of God's relationship with that creation and with us as his creatures. Of course we still have sins to confess – and sin is no more beautiful than it ever was – but we confess our sins from the perspective of a loved, though errant, child to a loving father, rather than from the perspective of potentially damned sinner to stern judge. The expressions of heartfelt sorrow and the burden of sin may still be validly used as being accurate reflections of our feelings about ourselves as sinners – many of us actually do feel this bad about our manifold shortcomings – but we need to re-interpret the words as being just this, an expression of our feelings, rather than as being a supposedly accurate statement (or at least inferral) of our beliefs about the nature of God and his relationship with us. The ancient words need consciously to be interpreted in the light of what we actually think and believe today, and the theological ideas to which we subscribe must be those of today (which stands as a kind of sub-text) rather than those of the 1549 or 1662 text itself.

A similar process of re-interpretation is required when we come to consider the language in which we make our intercessions, especially in the fixed form as required in the service of Holy Communion. There is no realistic method of circumventing this form, for it would be a serious liturgical *faut pas* to tamper with the 'Prayer for the Church Militant', and in this prayer we are confronted with a picture of God and his activity which is barely credible in a modern setting. Occasional (and unnecessary) changes are often made in the supposed interests of intelligibility – 'living' for 'lively' and 'impartially' for 'indifferently' (the second of these emendations being now actually enshrined in the text of the *Book of Common Prayer* 2004) – but the substance of the prayer is left unchanged, as is, very often one suspects, the theological framework which undergirds it, even though this framework is archaic in the extreme. As with the forms of confession, the words of this prayer may be allowed to remain (and few worshippers would not miss their sonorous beauty) but they must be read from within the context of a genuinely contemporary theological understanding rather than a sixteenth or seventeenth century one. Thus the various petitions of the prayer may still be understood as powerful expressions of our deepest hopes and desires – we do indeed passionately long for the comforting and succouring of those in adversity, and for the probity and rectitude of those who govern us – but we can no longer find these hopes exactly reflected in our understanding of how God acts in the world. Once again a modern theological sub-text is needed to enable us appropriately to interpret and to use afresh words which originated in a long-vanished theological world.

Having concentrated on the difficulties which are raised by the use of an ancient liturgy, it might be thought that a solution could readily be provided by the use of a modern form of worship. In theory this might indeed be the case, but in practice the problem all too often remains in contemporary language services and may even be exacerbated simply because lying behind the contemporary language are precisely the same theological pre-suppositions about the nature of God's activity as were there in the liturgy of some four-hundred-and-fifty years previously. We use what appears to be – because of its language – a liturgy which reflects and speaks to our contemporary condition, and therefore it is less readily open to re-interpretation than a liturgy which is patently that of a previous age. We are therefore faced with the ironic and uncomfortable need to re-interpret something which is not supposed to need any re-interpretation.

More specifically, then, what are some of the problems of belief and theology which arise even (and perhaps especially) in the use of 'modern' liturgies. Again there is a plethora of examples which might be cited, but for the sake of brevity I propose here to touch briefly on only two of them: the eucharistic theology involved in some of the prayers of consecration; and the use of scripture in the lectionary and the general method (and standard) of preaching on such passages of scripture.

The central problem is that the best of our theological thinking has moved on, especially in response to the intellectual upheavals of the past two centuries or so, but the faith of many believers has not, so that the church at large is still substantially in the grip of a pre-modern, and with it pre-critical, mind set. This creates a two-fold difficulty. For some, perhaps for many believers, there is no conscious discomfort involved – they are content to live within this mind-set and to conduct their religious life in the currency of a bygone age. But even this easy-going acceptance of the comfort of the familiar is not without its underlying conflicts both actual and potential; for there is an actual discrepancy between the way such people think of and address God (and the way in which he is often believed to act), and the ways in which we can coherently think of him and speak of him (and believe in his activity) in a post-modern age, and there is a further potential conflict between the old world and the new as soon as any individual believer realises themselves the chasm which exists between their faith and theological 'reality'. The resolution of this struggle and a move towards modernity demands much courage and the complete re-evaluation of all that is familiar, for it is far easier either to abandon faith or hide one's head in the sand than it is to discover that much of what has been held dear is thoroughly pernicious theologically and must be refined and purged in order to continue being worth the effort of belief. To move from the pre-modern to the post-modern demands an intellectual jump of two hundred or so years within the span of a single lifetime, and in the present climate it is surprising not that so few people manage to make that move, but that anyone should manage it at all!

The second difficulty exists not for those who are content to remain where they are, but for those who have made or are making the move from one theological age to another. In a church which has a predominantly pre-modern liturgy and mind-set, this is not a comfortable move. As soon as any conventional norms are challenged or a non-literal understanding of our prayers, worship or scripture is advocated, the cry of 'heresy' or 'atheism' goes up, and positions which would be wholly familiar and unthreatening to the theologian are condemned by the 'man in the pew' as too radical for his ears. The classic modern example of this would be the Rt Revd David Jenkins during his time as Bishop of Durham. Many of his ideas (long familiar in theological circles) were picked up in half-understood fragments and rejected by a large conservative body of opinion in the church. What was needed then, and is still needed today, is a much closer link between that theological world and the body of the church so that those who find themselves moving on theologically are reassured that it is not *de facto* a heresy to question even the best established theological proposition or to re-interpret familiar words. In our present state (liturgically speaking) we need to be encouraged and reassured to learn that good theology is not incompatible with inadequate words, so that we can understand the words we say as being a genuine expression of our own desires, whilst acknowledging that they do not necessarily provide an accurate representation of what we actually believe. For a few (and for most of the professionally committed) this has long been the case anyway. What is needed is that theology should come down to earth enough to make the redeeming knowledge of this freedom available to the many who are still inside their ancient prison and have not realised that theology has picked the lock of their prison long since!

Specifically, then, there is a mass (if that is the appropriate word!) of confusions and misinterpretations around when we stop seriously to consider much of our eucharistic language. Inevitably a good deal of this language, especially in the eucharistic prayers and in such associated passages as the *Agnus Dei*, is centred around our interpretation and understanding of the atonement, and thus the problem of eucharistic language substantially overlaps with the wider issue of how we might understand the atonement today. Put very briefly, the problem is a simple one in terms of definition, even if not of resolution. The reality of the atonement – that Jesus' death and resurrection inaugurated a new relationship between humanity and God and ushered in a radically new era – is not at issue. Instead, what is at issue is the question of precisely how we can understand and express that reality and that changed and renewed relationship. It is one thing to say something like 'Jesus died for me', and quite another to begin to explain coherently how one man's particularly savage death has brought about redemption for humanity.

Since this is not a treatise specifically on the doctrine of the atonement, there is not space here to enter exhaustively into every one of the many facets of the situation, and for the purposes of the present argument one particular illustration will suffice. Much of our eucharistic language, then, is centred either around the notion of 'sacrifice', or, even worse, around the model known as 'penal substitution'. Admittedly this chimes in perfectly with our conviction that 'Jesus died for me' (however we may wish to express that conviction), and it is entirely consonant with a constant thread running through two thousand years of Christian history. What is left unsaid, however, and therefore all too often left to the largely theologically untutored minds of the bulk of our congregations, is how this language of sacrifice or substitution is to be interpreted. For most people, I suspect, the possibility that such language is figurative does not occur. Our texts speak of sacrifice and so a sacrifice there must have been – and 'Jesus died for me' comes to mean that he died in my place, suffering a death he did not deserve in order to free me from a death which I do deserve. Even thus far this may still sound acceptable if taken purely at face value – and indeed we have said nothing more than the classic theory of substitutionary atonement says. But no theological statement stands entirely alone, and to say that Jesus was literally a sacrifice makes, by implication, a statement about God – namely that he required or demanded a sacrifice. And it is at this point that the theological waters become decidedly muddy, for whilst previous centuries may have been happy with this idea, it is one which sits rather uncomfortably in the moral climate of the present age, and one which threatens (for all the convoluted efforts of theologians to explain it away) to reduce God to a cruel tyrant, or at least a being whose forgiveness is harder to gain than is human forgivenness.

Once again then, there is a discrepancy between what we say in worship and what we actually believe – or at least would be most constructive for us to believe. For surely it would be appropriate to acknowledge that language such as that of sacrifice is not intended to be construed literally as representing the facts of what happened. Yes, it accurately depicts one facet of my feelings about the cross, in that it reminds me powerfully of my own unworthiness and sin, and of God's overwhelming goodness and love in delivering me from the burden of that sin, but it is essential to interpret it in this light (which has no further unfortunate theological consequences) rather than to attempt to build an understanding of the atonement which is overly, and dangerously literal.

These remarks form only the briefest sketch of the problem, but serve at least to indicate something of its scope. A considerably fuller treatment – together with an attempt to create a coherent modern interpretation of the atonement – may be found in *Don Cupitt and the Future of Christian Doctrine*,[1] and similarly, excellent discussions of the place and value of a variety of interpretations of the atonement are provided by William Marshall in the closing chapter of his book *The Passion of Christ*,[2] by Stephen Sykes in *The Story of Atonement*,[3] and by J. Denny

Weaver in *The Nonviolent Atonement*.[4] All of these discussions represent the kind of thinking which is so sorely needed today to bridge the gap between words and belief and to bring our ancient liturgies into life once more. We may still wish to use the words, categories and concepts of an earlier age, but the function of theology must be not to leave these unchanged and irrelevant, but to open up to us new ways of handling old concepts such that they once again can take root and blossom in a different cultural soil from that in which they were first planted.

Both of these areas of difficulty, the forms of intercession and the eucharistic language which we use, are of course in one sense 'givens' in our liturgy. They are printed in black and white, and any attempt at re-interpretation has to take the form, as has been stated already, of an implicit 'sub-text' in the light of which we understand afresh the words which we actually say.

This is not the case with the second of the aspects of our liturgy which I have chosen to examine, that of preaching, and the use made of scripture and theology in that preaching. It is ironic that this should be a problem at all, for here in preaching there exists what is potentially one of the most valuable links of all between the language of worship and the underlying framework of belief to which we assent. In preaching there is given, week by week, a chance to bridge some of the gaps which we have noted: to explain, to re-interpret and to make real and fresh for the twentieth century both the underlying truths and the changing dress of Christian theology and spirituality.

The irony, to which we have referred, is that this potential for easing the problem is all too often neglected, and that indeed, the practice of preaching often serves to widen the gaps between theology and worship and theology and the Christian life. One would not wish to be too sweeping: there are undoubtedly clergy (and lay readers) who in their preaching explore the content of faith for today and relate what we say and what we do and think in a meaningful fashion. At the same time, however, one is uncomfortably aware – simply on the basis of personal experience and the number of sermons one hears or reads – that this is by no means universally the case. More often one finds that a piece of scripture is treated in isolation and addressed purely on its own terms, with the result that a wedge is driven between the world of scripture (and any theological position founded on it) and the world of our everyday existence, and too many questions are begged concerning either the nature of God or of his activity in the world.

As an example of this one might well take one of the various miracles of Jesus which appear in the Sunday lectionary. With any of these miracles there are, for any thoughtful or critical believer, a number of prior considerations which need to be addressed before the episode can be questioned on its own terms. We need to establish our understanding of what happened (or may have happened) and to decide on what level we can interpret the story (literal, imaginative, metaphorical, parabolical etc) before we can intelligently ask what the story has to teach us in terms of our understanding of our faith. Much of the time, I would suggest, however, these questions are left unasked and unanswered in preaching, and it is simply assumed (or allowed to be assumed by default) that the story records exactly what happened, and that all that needs to be done is to draw from the story as it stands some 'moral' or pattern for our spiritual or ethical life.

Such a simplistic approach (both to scripture itself and to the vital task of preaching on it) begs the question of what we actually believe about the life, ministry, death and resurrection of Jesus, and creates an intellectual vacuum in which we may struggle in vain to explain why God appeared to be so active in Jesus and the apostles and appears, by contrast, to have been more or less quiescent ever since. It is surely both more creative and of greater potential relevance to our Christian life, to set any particular story in its context and to attempt to explain why the story was told in such-and-such a way. If scripture is approached in this fashion then we can elucidate both what the evangelist or other author was attempting to communicate about his own belief and the belief of his church or community, and also something of what that belief might mean for us today – and furthermore, in some cases, in what ways that belief might need to be re-interpreted or reformulated if it is to have meaning for us today at all.

Thus far we have simply raised and provided an exposition of some of the problems concerning the place (or lack of it) of theology in public worship. This is all very well – and it is important for the church to acknowledge that these problems exist – but the identification of problems presupposes the need for a solution to those problems. If then, as we have argued, these problems exist, what, if anything, can be done to address them?

It would require a full-length study of this one issue to answer this question in any fully adequate depth, but within the constraints of the wider framework of this study, four potential avenues of exploration may be identified, any or all of which might, if pursued, help to re-unite the often disparate realms of theology and public worship.

First, we may return to the notion of a divorce between the study of theology and the daily realities of Christian practice which we have explored already. The simple fact of there being such a divorce tends to isolate all theological productions – even those which might otherwise be creative and relevant – from the ongoing life of the church. A prime instance of this would be the fate of the reports of the Church of England Doctrine Commission during the past twenty years or so, and indeed the fate of all too many of the various inter-denominational reports of the same period. The Doctrine Commission, for example, has always, presumably, attempted to produce reports which will inform the life of the church, and the intent of the commission is to be directly of service to the church in its ministry and mission. To this end, the commission has produced a number of excellent reports in recent years such as *Believing in the Church* and *We Believe in God*, and yet it is highly questionable whether any of these reports (in spite of an often very creative understanding of God and especially of prayer) has had any real significant influence on the everyday life and worship of the vast bulk of the church. A first avenue, therefore, might be for the church to explore ways in which the relationship between the thinking and the practice of the church might be made more direct than at present, and to discover ways of ensuring that such excellent thinking as is contained in these reports (and in other works too, of course) actually does percolate down to and inform church life at the parochial and personal level. It might be, for example, that there is a role here for parochial or diocesan meetings to be held as a forum for the discussion of these and other theological reports just as such gatherings are already asked on occasions to consider issues of pastoral practice or church order.

Secondly, and it is itself part of this effort at directness and improved communication, there is a pressing need for the clergy (and other teachers) to make connections between theological thinking, worship and daily life precisely through the medium of their preaching and teaching. That this does not happen sufficiently may perhaps be attributable to a 'fear' of theology – or indeed of any serious in-depth critical study. It is often assumed by clergy that lay people will not be able to cope with such study: it will be above their heads, and will simply confuse or unsettle them. To make such an assumption is, however, to underestimate and effectively to patronise lay people. There is, too, the further possibility that clergy patronise lay people in this way in order to conceal another and deeper fear – that lay people may indeed actually be able to cope with such theological matters, and may threaten the position of the clergy by proving themselves to be in due course their theological equals. Whatever the reason may be, though, such a patronising attitude is patently untenable. It may well be true that anyone starting 'from scratch' as it were, would not be able to read with much profit a seven hundred page tome on the atonement for example, but this should not be equated with theological illiteracy. On the contrary, many people are well able to respond to intelligent and stretching thinking about God and his activity, and this response will then be reflected in their attitudes towards, and manner of worship. Lest this should sound like merely a pious

hope I would add that I have seen this work in practice in parish
life, and it is appropriate to say a word or two here in appreciation of a parish which taught me this particular lesson. I served
for four and a half years in the remote parish of Gweedore,
Templecrone and Carrickfinn on the western seaboard of Co.
Donegal, and in response to the parishioners' (mainly sheep
farmers) own request a bible study group was set up. This ran
from October to April each year and had a healthy core member-
ship of ten or twelve. The group began with a course – in some
detail – on biblical scholarship and criticism, and then proceeded
in the succeeding years to look at a variety of biblical texts in the
light of this theological understanding of scripture, and along
the way there were frequent digressions to explore some particular theological point which emerged in the course of our reading. The discoveries and enthusiasm of this group were then
often reflected in sermons (which could be themselves quite
stretching thanks to this background of study) and in the conduct of our worship. The parishioners of Gweedore, Templecrone and Carrickfinn (and of other parishes too, no doubt) are a
living proof that connections can be made between theology, life
and worship at a parish level, and of the simple fact that such
connections need to be made more often if both theology itself
and the church's life and worship are to thrive.

A third avenue which might be pursued is that of reciprocity
between the thinking of liturgists and theologians. Certainly
each have their own specialised spheres of interest, but this
should not obscure the implicit relationship between them, and
good liturgy and good theology need to renew their covenant
with each other in each successive generation. At the risk of incurring the wrath of liturgists and theologians alike, I would
suggest that this has by no means always happened. The language of worship in every tradition has been modernised – in
part at least, and either more or less successfully according to
one's taste – but there is little or no reflection of changed (and
still changing) patterns of thought, hence the problems which
we have considered here. As any liturgical volume comes to-

wards the end of its scheduled life, the air becomes full of discussion as to the possibility – and content – of another new prayer book or missal, and this raises the question once again of what the governing principles of its editing and authorship will be. Will a desire for traditional ideas and forms dominate, or will ways be found to cast the best of our contemporary thinking into acceptable and beautiful liturgical forms? One would hope that the latter course might prevail, and there is in the modern language Church of Ireland rite (as the inevitable exception which proves the rule) one prayer of modern origin which indicates that this can be done successfully. The prayer to which I refer is the first of the two post-communion prayers, intended to be said by the priest alone, but frequently said by the congregation also, no doubt on account of its richness and beauty:

Father of all,
we give you thanks and praise,
that when we were still far off
you met us in your Son and brought us home.
Dying and living, he declared your love,
gave us grace, and opened the gate of glory.
May we who share Christ's body live his risen life;
we who drink his cup bring life to others;
we whom the Spirit lights give light to the world.
Keep us firm in the hope you have set before us,
so that we and all your people shall be free,
and the whole earth live to praise your name;
through Christ our Lord.

Beauty, prayer, liturgy and theology, it appears, may yet walk hand in hand.

The fourth and final avenue of exploration is a more general one which in a sense overarches the specific areas which we have indicated thus far. It is simply to bring to consciousness within the church the need to ensure that the ways in which we address God and the things we say about him in our worship actually do reflect accurately the ways in which we think of him –

in other words it is not only liturgists and theologians who must dwell on this issue, but rather it is one which needs the engagement of the whole church, such that it is the body of the church which finds a contemporary voice for its worship and not merely a select few who forge ahead, leaving the bulk of the faithful still in the liturgical dark ages. Such a serious engagement will require openness and courage on the part of the church. It may make our worship more 'open-ended', more challenging and less cosily certain of God's direct activity in the world; but ultimately it would make that worship more creative and uplifiting as we get to grips with the kind of God we actually do believe in rather than the kind of God we used to believe in or the kind of God we would prefer not to believe in – which is so often at present the case.

All of these avenues might profitably be explored by the church, and there may well be others also, and hopefully the kind of developments indicated here will prove both possible and fruitful. But worship, though central, is only one aspect of the church's existence. Thus far we have left untouched the equally vast area of private prayer, and clearly this is likewise centrally constitutive of our spiritual identity and expectations, and to this realm of private prayer we must now therefore turn.

CHAPTER THREE

Theology and Private Prayer

It is evident that at some level or another, whether adequately or not, our theology is intimately connected with our public worship: it is after all in our corporate weekly or daily worship as the church that we employ the classical formulations of the Apostles' and Nicene Creeds, and attempt at least to give expression to the deepest collective insights and aspirations of the church. Public worship is the means by which the church most obviously articulates its own identity, not only to itself but also to the world, and it is therefore hardly surprising that what we believe should in that context be equally as important as the precise words and concepts through which we express those beliefs.

In the case of private prayer the connection may be less evident, and it may be more surprising, therefore, that we have chosen to associate theology and private prayer so closely. It may be thought that whilst we may require the framework which theology provides to give form and shape to our corporate worship, yet when we are alone and in private communion with God we are – or should be – free from such outward constraints and at liberty to commune with God in whatever words, positions and mental attitudes we may happen to find most meaningful.

At one level, of course, this is true. In our private devotions we are obviously not subject to the same constraints which apply in most, if not all, of our public worship. We are not required to follow a fixed form or repeat any set form of words, and we come to private prayer with whatever mental and spiritual attitude, awareness and receptivity we may happen to have at that particular time, an attitude which, unlike that with which we approach public worship, is not moulded by the knowledge that we are in communion with others just as much as with God. Our time, our attitude and our prayers are, in a profound sense, which is not necessarily true of public worship, our own.

But to acknowledge all of this is by no means to say that we are free from any and every theological framework, or that we approach God afresh each time *in vaccuo*. For however free we may feel on any occasion, the truth is that we come to our prayers from within our ongoing spiritual life which is (and always has been) moulded both by the theological aspects of public worship and by our own personal apprehension and understanding of the theological tradition of Christianity. As John Burnaby remarked in *Soundings*, it is inevitable that, 'the praying of the Christian, when he enters into his chamber and shuts his door, should be influenced in both form and content by the prayers in which he has joined in Church.'[1] We may not think consciously about theology when first we bend our knees, but as soon as our mind or our mouth begins to stutter the first words of our prayers, we shall find ourselves living and thinking within a definite framework of theological thought. That framework may very well be unconscious, but that does not make it one whit the less powerful. The framework that we bring to our prayers (whether consciously or unconsciously) will profoundly inform the whole manner of our praying: how we address God; what precise form our prayers take; what response we expect and what we understand by an 'answer' to prayer. Stated baldly in this fashion this may perhaps seem a far-fetched claim and an over-assessment of the potency of theology. According to even such an eminent scholar as Alister McGrath, however, theology, and with it specific doctrinal positions, is fundamentally constitutive both of how we think and therefore of how we behave – prayer included. He comments with justified acerbity as he contrasts the impact of Christian doctrines with those of other ideologies:

> Marxist values rest upon Marxist doctrines, such as the non-existence of God and the inevitability of socialism – just as

Christian values ultimately rest upon Christian doctrines. A
failure to realise the extent to which values, attitudes and actions rest upon doctrinal foundations explains much of the
moral shallowness of Christian liberalism in recent years.[2]

Theology, then, is intimately connected with all that we think or
do, and our assumptions and beliefs, whether overtly expressed
or not, therefore clearly have the power either to free us or
shackle us in our converse with God.

Most of the theological assumptions which we bring to
prayer will be concerned with the nature of God himself and
with his activity, and it therefore seems appropriate to explore
the realm of private prayer through the medium of one particular doctrine, that of the Holy Trinity – although this will inevitably entail also some consideration of other associated doctrines such as the Incarnation.

First though, it is important to attempt to establish, in outline
at least, what a basic understanding of prayer might be. Why do
we pray? And what are we doing (or what do we think we are
doing) when we pray? It may be that, put as simply as this, these
questions seem naïve, and yet they are nonetheless fundamental, and our answers to them will profoundly influence both our
attitude towards, and the content of our prayers. For this reason,
if for no other, these apparently simplistic questions deserve at
least some sort of an answer.

Why, then, do we pray? At the outset it may be predicated
that the answer to this question is likely to involve a complex
amalgam of subjective and objective, proactive and reactive,
need and response. Thus, as far as need is concerned, there is
likely to be, at the heart of our praying, something which finds
an echo in Schliermacher's 'feeling of absolute dependence'. We
probably would not wish to go as far as Schliermacher in ascribing to this feeling all of the roots of our religious quest and
experience, and yet there is undoubtedly something of truth in
this attitude for our understanding of prayer. What Schliermacher experiences as the governing characteristic of our entire
religious life has been reflected in the language of prayer again

and again, from Augustine's conviction that 'our hearts are rest-less until they find their rest in thee', to the sentiments of the Second Collect at Morning Prayer that we have to do with a God 'whose service is perfect freedom'. Regardless of the possible ex-cesses of Schliermacher's position, it would nonetheless appear to be a perennial feature of the Christian spiritual tradition that our recourse to prayer is indeed an expression of our deepest and most profound needs – however haltingly expressed, or in-deed inexpressible, these may turn out to be.

But there is surely more to prayer than an expression of human need, which, powerful and emotive though it may be, may yet turn out to be something entirely subjective and bearing little or no relationship to reality – although, of course a strong case can be made that such need does indeed bear a direct rela-tionship to reality.[3] It is merely that however well-substantiated this relationship to reality may be, it is not enough if prayer is perceived as being rooted solely in the human psyche.

Beyond this, therefore, we believe as Christians that prayer is an expression of our human response both to a divine command and to a divine initiative. It is an attempt on our part to respond to the love which we know to have first loved us and to have called us to a response. Furthermore, it is a direct response to the divine command and teaching of Jesus, and to the example of Jesus himself.

But there is more to prayer even than this though. Even the desire to pray – and of course, following it, the act of praying it-self – is an expression of the will concerning the whole orienta-tion of our existence. Prayer (in addition to the elements already mentioned, and maybe many more which we have left un-touched) is a statement of intent, an articulation of the desire that our human will should be moulded and shaped by contact with (and indeed ultimately union with) the divine will.

These then might be at least some of the reasons for which, and attitudes in which we come to prayer; but if the why of prayer is important, so too is the what. When we pray, what is it that we understand ourselves as doing? What are we attempting to 'achieve' by it, and what expectations do we have concerning the nature of God's response to our prayers? What is, if you like, 'going on' when we pray?

Part of the answer to these questions is obviously closely related to the reasons why we pray which we have already outlined. Thus in prayer we do understand ourselves to be expressing our deepest needs and aligning our will and being with God's in response to his initiative towards us. Further than this, though, a wide variety of other answers have been returned to the question of what we are doing when we pray – and these answers are by no means necessarily mutually exclusive.

A part of the church's life of prayer then, is prayer of the contemplative or meditative variety, which, although they are strictly speaking different 'methods' of prayer, will be treated together here for the sake of simplicity. This type of prayer has always been an important element in the life of many religious communities, and even if long undervalued by the wider church is gaining increasing recognition today as a viable and rich way of prayer, perhaps especially through the pioneering work of Robert Coulson and the Fellowship of Contemplative Prayer which he founded in 1949. Prayer of this sort (which may involve simple stillness, or the contemplation of an object or a phrase of scripture, or gentle repetition of such a phrase, and which has always been a part of Eastern Orthodox spirituality through such prayers as the 'Jesus Prayer') may be characterised as being principally a waiting upon God, a waiting which can then be extended beyond fixed times of prayer into something approaching Brother Lawrence's 'practice of the presence of God'. The intention of such prayer is to rid the mind of all its usual distractions and 'open up' the channels of communication such that we may learn to hear the 'still small voice' of God himself. There is no 'agenda' in such prayer, and we do not approach God with particular petitions in contemplation. Rather, we are silent, inwardly and outwardly and our communication with God is through that silence which we offer to him that he might fill it with himself.

At the other end of the spectrum – though by no means incompatible with a contemplative approach to prayer – are the
more fully verbalised forms of prayer, of which the most obvious would be, perhaps, intercession. Intercession, as we shall
see, is all too frequently misunderstood as far as both intention
and efficacy are concerned. For intercession (properly understood) is not about making demands of God, or even about attempting to persuade God to respond in particular ways.
Rather, it is in Michael Ramsey's felicitious and evocative
phrase, a being 'with God with the people on our heart'.[4] We are
not bargaining with God or seeking to change his mind: we are
simply offering to him a person or a situation together with our
own concern and compassion, and trusting in his loving will to
respond by whatever means and in whatever way may, as the
prayer of St Chrysostom puts it, 'be most expedient' for us.
Indeed, far from seeking to persuade God into a particular
course of action, a part of our intention in intercessory prayer
must be to open up our own minds and wills to whatever response God sees fit to make, and to seek the grace to learn something of his purpose and his love as we endeavour to understand and interpret that response. There is thus the same openness and receptivity involved in intercessory prayer as there is
in contemplative prayer, and the practice of the one does not, as
we have said, exclude the other.

Clearly, though, contemplative prayer and intercession are
not the only forms of prayer. We have not touched on, for example, adoration or confession, nor indeed is this necessary, for I
would simply argue that whatever variety or mode of prayer we
may engage in, the primary necessity is for this fundamental attitude of openness and receptivity. It is axiomatic in the life of
prayer that whilst what we want to say to God may be important, what God has to say to us is more important still, and a large
part of our prayer must consist in our readiness to receive God's
self-communication to us.

If receptivity is one of the underlying constituents of our
praying, then I would suggest that the other fundamental re-

quirement – intimately connected with it – is that our praying is
always from within a position of trusting hopefulness. As we pray
we turn in faith and hope to the God whom we perceive as the
source of all things. Our trusting hopefulness in prayer is a kind of
existential application of Julian of Norwich's vision that, 'All shall
be well, and all shall be well, and all manner of thing shall be well'.
In and through our praying we learn to believe the truth of this
ultimate confidence – even if we cannot, for whatever reason, always experience or understand it now. Perhaps this absolute trust,
this sense that 'underneath are the everlasting arms' cannot even
ever quite be put into words: it is almost too profound for mere
words, since it is our total attitudinal response (mental, spiritual
and emotional) to the one whom we believe to be the source of all
life, all hope, all meaning. We cannot adequately verbalise the
nature of this trust, and neither (and very importantly) can we adequately predict God's response to our trust, save that it will be
one of love: we cannot enter prayer certain of what God will or will
not do. In the end we are simply offering ourselves to God's perfect love and perfect will in an act of utter faith, a faith that whatever God may or may not do and whatever may befall us of good
or of ill, the reality of God (whatever we ultimately may find that
to mean) is, and will be for eternity, better than any spurious reality
which may deny or ignore him.

It may appear that this is rather a frail and faltering account
of prayer, but I cannot help but feel that this is likely to be true of
any account which attempts to do justice to the majesty and
mystery of the God with whom we have to do in our praying. It
is better to stutter a little before the glory of God than to be too
sure of ourselves and then discover that the being to whom we
are addressing our prayers is merely ourselves writ large, or a
shrunken caricature of God whom we have created for ourselves to be more nearly on our own level. Such a God may feel
safer than the real God, but he is safer only because he can do
nothing. We might do well to remember in all of our praying
that, 'It is a terrible thing to fall into the hands of the living God',
and that as C. S. Lewis memorably put it: 'Safe?˜Who said any-

thing about safe? 'Course he isn't safe. But he's good. He's the King, I tell you.'[5]

As we attempt to articulate any account of prayer, then, we should bear in mind that, as even this brief excursus has reminded us, prayer is an activity at once complex and profound and, importantly, an activity whose consequences are, in the best sense of the phrase, beyond us. In the light of this, the disturbing thing about so much of our prayer (and, I am sure, in private as well as in public) is that it is of what might be called the 'shopping-list' variety – in other words prayer which is of a naïvely intercessory kind and which often seems to presuppose a directly interventionist God who may be persuaded or manipulated by our prayers. Perhaps it should be acknowledged that this may not always be the intention behind the prayer, but it is certainly what is overtly stated in much of the language of prayer.

Furthermore, the other (and perhaps even more disturbing) feature of much of this simplistic petitionary prayer is that it is lop-sided in terms of any Trinitarian balance. As the Doctrine Commission of the Church of England recognised, any real depth of understanding of the Trinity is lacking for most people:

> … the majority of Christians in the West today, it must be admitted, would be hard pressed even to give an account, let alone a defence, of the developed doctrine of the Trinity as expressed in Christianity's historic creeds and the documents of its Councils.[6]

This imbalance may take one of two forms, and both of them are equally damaging to a genuine Trinitarian understanding of God. For many people (and I can only base this observation on the pastoral experience of listening to people talking about their prayer over a period of slightly over two decades) prayer is addressed solely to 'God'. It may be formally 'through Jesus Christ', but it is so in name only. The reality is that it is addressed to a somewhat monolithic God whose attributes or persons are not seriously distinguished. Jesus Christ may be invoked almost by way of courtesy at the conclusion of a prayer, and the Holy Spirit is often totally neglected.

By contrast, there is the characteristic mode of prayer of what is often called the 'charismatic' element in the church. I have no wish unfairly to caricature this dimension of the church's life, but perhaps it would be true to say that the major emphasis within the charismatic movement is on 'life in the Spirit', with all that that entails by way of spiritual gifts, and that charismatic prayer tends at least to be a reflection of this overriding concern with the things of the Spirit. As far as prayer is concerned, this has almost the opposite result of the approach we have just described. Charismatic prayer would tend to be centred around the invocation of the Holy Spirit. With this there runs, to a greater or lesser extent, an association with the person of Jesus Christ – although this will depend on how far the overt association is made between Jesus himself and the Holy Spirit as the medium of the risen and ascended Christ's ongoing presence in the life of the church. But whether or not this connection is made, what is frequently completely lacking is any meaningful recognition of God as Father. In charismatic prayer the first person of the Trinity is often almost or entirely neglected. Coming from someone who is outside the charismatic movement, this may sound like an overly sweeping and derogatory statement, and it is therefore instructive to note that one leading member of this dimension of the church's life has written a book with the arresting title, *The Forgotten Father,* his thesis being precisely that:

> If I were to diagnose and prescribe for its [the charismatic movement's] present ills in a single sentence, I would say that it needs to know the Father,[7]

to which he adds that:

> Precisely at this stage in its development it needs the correction and direction that would be given to it by a concentration on these aspects of the Christian message that gather round the person, nature and work of God the Father.[8]

If these two pictures are at all true, and if it is the case that, for different reasons, much of our prayer is insufficiently Trinitarian in its roots and emphasis, then we might usefully examine in some depth our understanding of God as Trinity and consider what this might suggest to us about God and his activity, especially in the realm of prayer and answers to prayer. In other words, we might do well, for our own spiritual health, to seek to elucidate what our most basic Christian doctrine – God as Trinity – suggests about our most basic Christian activity – that of prayer.

It is in keeping with Tom Smail's timely reminder, as well as in accord with the church's understanding of the Father as being the first person of the Trinity, that we should begin by considering at least briefly (if it is not considered too sexist to dwell on it at all), what implications the Fatherhood of God might have for our life of prayer. And the first thing which needs to be said about the Christian understanding of God as Father, or indeed, if we use inclusive language, as Mother – which might seem self-evident and naïve were it not so all too rarely apparent in practice – is that it at once brings a directly relational dimension into our prayer. This was reinforced for me some years ago, when at a Diocesan Clergy Conference the Bishop of Tuam, the Rt Revd Richard Henderson reminded us pertinently that the Father is only the Father in so far as he is the Father of the Son, the Son is the Son only in so far as he is the Son of the Father, and the Holy Spirit is not a free-floating entity, but the Holy Spirit of God. Our prayer, then, is addressed neither to an impersonal God, nor even to a personal God with whom we have no specific relationship other than that of creature to creator, but to a God whom it is our privilege confidently, through the prior Sonship of Jesus, to address as 'Abba, Father'.

The fact that prayer is thus a relational activity is far more than a mere disinterested statement about how prayer 'functions': it is something which fundamentally and profoundly shapes our whole attitude to prayer. It does so, I would suggest, in three ways especially.

First, it both provides and requires an intimacy in prayer. The addressing of a deity is not necessarily an intimate business; but the relationship of Father and child in which we have been placed and into which we learn to grow is one of remarkable intimacy. It suggests a vulnerability (on both sides) and a capacity to be affected and moved which is totally absent from a simple divine potentate/human supplicant model. Furthermore it both suggests and requires (if the Father/child relationship is to become a reality) a heartfelt depth of involvement and commitment on our part just as much as on God's. Prayer is the reaching out of the whole person and demands our fullest self-offering. It is far more than something which is merely pragmatic or which can be reduced to a fixed form of words: it is ultimately about my entering into relationship with another, with all of the vulnerability and risks, as well as all of the creative potential and joy which this entails. To say 'Abba, Father' is at least as much to make a statement about myself as it is to make a statement about God.

Secondly, and following directly from this all-pervading intimacy, it becomes true that prayer and the relationship which it feeds become something much more than a ritual performed at fixed times or in purely formal words. Prayer and the relationship which is rooted in it spills over into the whole of life. Our relationship with God is an ongoing one, not a stop-start affair in which we meet him only at set times and in set places. Certainly there may be special times and places of meeting (as in any other relationship) but the relationship, and with it the communication, is there all the time.

Thirdly, the character of this Father/child relationship shapes our attitude to prayer, for the predominant atmosphere of our prayer is not one of fear or any attempt to placate God, but rather, as we have commented in a different context already, one of trust and hope, of love and obedience. This is not to say that any element of power and authority is altogether neglected. Far from it; our relationship with God is, amongst other things, one of filial obedience to his divine authority, but it is an obedience grounded in love and trust rather than in fear or subservience.

The Fatherhood of God, then, shapes our approach to prayer

and sets the basic parameters within which that life of prayer is conducted, and through it we are encouraged to come to prayer in love and trust, looking to God's creative and redeeming love and seeing our prayer as being at once an expression of, and a growth in, our relationship with God.

The Fatherhood of God also, and inevitably, has consequences when we move on to consider the Second Person of the Trinity in connection with our prayer, for here again the keynote is one of relationship. Again it is almost so obvious as to go unnoticed that the fact of the Father/Son relationship between the First and Second Persons of the Trinity powerfully moulds our own attitude to prayer. Presumably it would be possible to offer prayer to a God who had three (or any other number) of 'faces' or 'persons' which had no organic relationship with one another except that they were different expressions of one reality. But such a prayer would be an entirely different experience from our prayer to God as Trinity. Thus there is a rich web of relationship into which we are drawn which colours our prayer life from the beginning. We know ourselves to be in a Father/child relationship; we see also the unique Father/Son relationship, and we can appropriate to ourselves by extension the closeness of that relationship such that we know ourselves adopted as children in a new sense through that primary Father/Son relationship, and also incorporated as brothers and sisters into the life of God himself through his Son.

But the Sonship of Jesus Christ is not the only feature of significance for our prayer. Again, it might theoretically be possible for there to be a Father/Son relationship within the deity which had no direct working out in the context of a human life – although it is hard to see what significance such a relationship might have for us, or even how we might come to apprehend it. However, the definitive act of the Son was his assumption of human form in the person of Jesus of Nazareth, and in the Incarnation there are profound implications for our faith and for our prayer. The doctrine of the Incarnation is one which we need to recover in all its power, not least for our understanding of prayer. That our faith is incarnational is axiomatic in so far as it is reflected in our sacramental worship and a more general sacramental approach to life on the part of the Christian faith, but there are other implications also which we will examine in detail later.

For the present, I propose simply to indicate certain ways in which our response to the Incarnate Son informs our prayer life at the outset. Clearly, as we have mentioned, we have in Jesus Christ an example for prayer, as well as, in the Lord's Prayer, a 'pattern' for prayer. In him we have the confidence to bring the whole of our frail human lives before God in the knowledge that we follow in the footsteps of one who is not remote from us, but is like us 'in every respect, except without sin'. Perhaps most of all though, we have the knowledge of his own trusting obedience in prayer, and the transforming vision through the cross and resurrection that God may be present and most active (as Luther discovered in his theology of the cross) precisely at the point at which he is perceived as being most absent. Just as Jesus felt abandoned by God, so we too may feel abandoned and alone at times, especially in times of stress or darkness. But exactly as the perception of God was hidden from Jesus on the cross (and from the onlookers too, we might add), but was in reality present most powerfully, so too in our prayers we are encouraged to know that in a very real sense our life is 'hid with Christ in God', and that from our human perspective we cannot entirely see the direction even of our own life and certainly not the complete manner of God's work within it. In our prayer, as in the rest of our life, we have rather the vision and the triumph of Jesus' death and resurrection to inspire us and uphold us to trust in the loving and redeeming will of God for us even in despair, pain or darkness.

So through the Incarnation the picture of our prayer life is rounded out still further, and the relationships within it become personalised in a human form. Yet even this is not enough, for it still leaves us with relationships which, if powerfully affective, are yet still ones for which we have to strive alone. It is all the more remarkable then that this is not, from the point of view of Christian doctrine, the end of the story. We are not left to reach out and strive after a God, who, however close he may be, is still 'out there'. For the doctrine of the Holy Spirit speaks of a God who is as much 'in here' as he is 'out there', and in this notion of indwelling, explored so powerfully and movingly in St John's gospel, all the potential richness of the relationships we have considered springs into life and is brought within our grasp.

I have no wish to enter into a long and learned discussion of the finer points of the doctrine of the Holy Spirit – the 'how' and the 'why' of his procession (single or double) or the exact nature of relationships within the Trinity, but merely to indicate why it is that this doctrine (however it is interpreted in its precise details) is so crucial to our life of prayer. In this less technical and more general sense, then, it is true to say that at the heart of the doctrine of the Holy Spirit is the notion of the Spirit as the ongoing and indwelling presence of the Risen Christ (and through him of the Father also) in the life both of the church and of the individual believer. Thus both as individuals and as the church we do not merely pray to God, but we also have the divine life as a dynamic presence within us.

If this is the case then our prayers become something more than our own unaided efforts. It is not surprising then – though it is never less than bewildering and awe-inspiring – to find St Paul writing of the Holy Spirit as one who prays in us, alongside us and through us, in 'sighs too deep for words'. Our thoughts and words may falter and even fail, but precisely at the point at which our human resources prove hopelessly inadequate, there is God himself, through his Holy Spirit, living out our halting prayers within us and transforming our inadequacy into the language of divinity itself. Through the Holy Spirit then, our prayer becomes something internal as well as external, motivated and conducted in us not merely by our own efforts and desires but by God himself. Our prayer becomes a conversation, a being with and a listening to, the God who by his Holy Spirit already indwells us: a discovery of the God who already lies at the heart of all that we are. Prayer is at once from us to God, but also through us both from and to the God who is already present within.

Again, parts of this account may seem inadequate or insufficiently defined, but I can only stress that some such perspective as this – that we are 'prayed in' as much as praying – is a perennial conviction in Christian spirituality throughout the ages. Indeed the strength of this conviction is powerfully endorsed by the 1987 Church of England Doctrine Commission report, *We Believe in God*. It might be thought that in our predominantly rationalistic age some other account of prayer might be looked for. It is instructive, however, that the Commission set its entire discussion of prayer in the context of God as Trinity, and spoke both passionately and eloquently of this sense of the Holy Spirit as the indwelling source of our prayer:

> Usually it dawns bit by bit on the person praying that this activity, which at first seems all one's own doing, is actually the activity of another. It is the experience of being 'prayed in', the discovery that 'we do not know how to pray as we ought' (Rom 8:26), but are graciously caught up in a divine conversation, passing back and forth in and through the one who prays, 'the Spirit himself bearing witness with our spirit' (Rom 8:16). We come to prayer empty-handed, aware of weakness, inarticulacy and even of a certain hollow 'fear and trembling', yet it is precisely in these conditions (cf 1 Cor 2:3-4) that divine dialogue flows. Here then is a way of beginning to understand what it might be to talk of the distinctiveness of the Spirit. It is not that the Spirit is being construed as a divine centre of consciousness entirely separate from the Father, as if two quite different people were having a conversation. Nor, again, is the Spirit conceived as the relationship between two entities that one can assume to be fixed (the Father and the person praying), a relationship which is then perhaps somewhat arbitrarily personified. Rather, and more mysteriously, the Spirit is here seen as that current of divine response to divine self-gift in which the one who prays is

caught up and thereby transformed (see again Rom 8:9-27, 1 Cor 2:9-16).[9]

Even from this comparatively brief survey, then, it appears that authentic Christian prayer is rooted in this conviction and experience of God as Trinity. Surprising though it may initially appear, especially in view of our earlier comments on how it may all too easily become irrelevant to us, theology is at the heart of our spiritual life. The final question to which we must address ourselves, therefore, is how does this appreciation of God as Trinity affect not merely our attitude towards prayer, but our whole understanding of it? How might we approach it and what might we expect of it if God and our relationship with him are as we have depicted them?

First, and perhaps most importantly, our understanding of God should lead us to a greater appreciation of the role of contemplative and meditative prayer. Instead of assuming that the bedrock of prayer is talking to God, we might find it truer to say that the foundation of prayer is listening to God. This would more accurately reflect our perception that we are the place of, and the recipient of prayer just as much as we are its begetter, and it might allow the life of prayer to be conducted within us rather than us feeling that it is something which we 'do' – often alone and unaided. For as Harry Williams discovered in his spiritual journey: 'God is both other than I am and also the same. For God is apprehended as the source from which I continually flow, and the source cannot be separated from that which continually flows from it.'[10]

Such a basic approach to prayer would rule out from the start any attempt to manipulate God, and prayer then becomes primarily the expression of our desire to be with God and to be the medium of what I have elsewhere called 'the silence of divine speech'.[11]

What then of intercession and all of the other more direct and consciously verbal forms of prayer? These, I would suggest, are not ruled out at all: indeed they remain as important as ever. They are simply transformed by being conducted from within

the governing framework of this more listening than demanding approach, and it is likewise from within this framework that
our answers to prayer should be expected.

But what sort of answers? In an approach to prayer in which
we appear to have more or less ruled out an externally and inde-
pendently interventionist kind of a God (whose actions we may
yet influence) what, if it does not mean an 'answer to prayer' in
the conventional sense, does the concept of God's response to
our prayer mean?

At the outset I would suggest that it means two things, both
of which are dependent upon and entirely consistent with the
account of prayer which we have outlined here, and both of
which have their roots in the notion of God as exercising his
Godhead not merely externally but through the medium of indwelling and Incarnation. The fullness of the Trinity is reflected
in the inter-relationship of the indwelling of the Holy Spirit, the
Incarnation of the Son and the authority of the Father.

First, then, there is the notion that even our prayers of request arise out of a primary attitude of listening, and therefore
we might expect answers to be received precisely through the
medium of that listening. Similarly, as all of our prayers are inspired by (and in a very real sense prayed by) the indwelling
Holy Spirit, so too we should not be surprised that answers to
prayer are often received by this same means as the life of God
himself flows in our praying from Spirit to Son and Father and
back again. Thus we may often find either that we are the answer to our own prayer, or that (and it is a slightly different
thing) we are the place within which our prayer is answered.

It is, I think, Metropolitan Anthony who provides one of the
most graphic examples of the former possibility. He describes an
occasion on which he had been praying passionately for a certain situation, and recounts his own discomfiture when he knew
himself to have receieved an answer: 'Well done, my son, you
have seen the need. Now go and do something about it.' Prayer,
in this instance, was for him the means of discovering his own
capability and being empowered to meet precisely the need for

which he had been praying. Such a response to prayer is clearly not always comfortable. It is much easier to hope that someone else will turn out to be the means of God answering our prayer, but if we will only listen for it then I suspect that the answer which Metropolitan Anthony received may not be infrequent.

In the latter case, we are, as I have put it, the place *within which*, rather than the means *by which* our prayer is answered. By this I mean that we ourselves are changed as a result of our prayer, and that this change is itself the answer – or perhaps at least a part of the answer – to our prayer. Thus, through prayer, I may be given a new vision or understanding of a person or situation; I may be enabled to find compassion or love where previously there was none; I may be shown how to act or speak in difficult circumstances and so on. Nothing external may have changed, but if I was myself a part of the situation or problem about which I have prayed, then it may well be that in changing me God has answered my prayer and facilitated the resolution of the problem.

This kind of answer to prayer again springs from the indwelling of the Holy Spirit, but in recognising my own place in the things for which I have prayed, it also invokes the principle of the Incarnation – in this instance in the fact that I am myself incarnated in a particular place and time and set of circumstances whose outcome I can influence. And this leads on to the second of the inferences for the answering of prayer which may be drawn from our discussion of God as Trinity.

We have seen, then, that God can act through the presence of his Holy Spirit within, and it can therefore be assumed that it is equally 'in character' for God to act incarnationally today just as he did uniquely in himself in the person of his Son. As far as answers to prayer are concerned, then, it is reasonable to expect that they may often come through the agency of other people – who may of course be motivated to act in such-and-such a way by the presence of the Holy Spirit within them and their prayers. This is in no way to suggest a reductionist understanding of prayer which downplays the activity of God himself. It is merely to suggest that God is most likely to act in ways which are in keeping with his own revealed nature. Something is no less an answer to prayer if it comes through another human being than it would be if it dropped 'ready made' from heaven. This is somewhat like a more theological version of the delightful old story of the man floundering in the sea following a shipwreck. When offered a lifebelt he replied, 'No. God will save me', and made the same response when given the opportunity of rescue first by a lifeboat and then by a helicopter. Having duly drowned, the man appeared in heaven and berated God: 'Why didn't you save me after I had shown such faith?' 'My child', God replied, 'I sent you a lifebelt, a lifeboat and a helicopter. What more did you expect me to do?' A useful parallel would be that of God as creator: we do not need to be biblical fundamentalists to hold a doctrine of creation, since God's creative activity is no less remarkable over a period of tens of billions of years and through the medium of a 'big bang' and evolution, than it is in the mythical seven days of Genesis. A natural agency – in this case a human one – does not exclude divine activity: indeed, given the doctrine of the Incarnation, it is precisely what we might expect.

In the course of this survey we have quite deliberately approached prayer from a theological standpoint, believing that what we think about our prayer and how we pray is, whether we know it or not, actually governed by our appreciation of theology. It therefore seems to make sense to attempt to ensure that the theology with which we approach prayer is coherent and consistent rather than otherwise. The picture of both theology and prayer which we have outlined here is, I believe, both coherent and consistent, although it may differ somewhat from many more 'popular' – and certainly from any more fundamentalist – understandings.

However, perhaps the best way to illustrate both its difference from such accounts and its greater coherence is to suggest a model for our prayer. Models – as all scientists are aware – must be used with care. They are never exact representations and they can never be exhaustive, and the similarities between model and reality should never (exactly as with allegory) be pushed too far or the result may well become a caricature.

That much said, however, the model which suggests itself for so much of our private prayer, and which I have several times heard directly recommended from the pulpit, is that of the telephone conversation. Without wishing to transgress against my own warnings and push this model too far, it seems obvious that this model has several major shortcomings. It is entirely mechanical and impersonal, and even the contact which is achieved by it is not a full personal contact but only that of disembodied voices which are finally disconnected, and it leaves all the onus of prayer firmly on our own doorstep. We are the sole initiators of the phone call, and the call is made to an entity entirely outside of (and remote from) ourselves.

If such a mechanical model appears to be inadequate, perhaps a more fruitful understanding may be found in a more organic image. Rather than a somewhat impersonal telephone conversation, the model which I find reflects most accurately the concept of God as at once 'beyond' and 'within' is the model of the child in the womb. Our prayer is akin to the circulation of the blood between mother and child. As with the child, there is a sense in which all the initiative and potential for life comes from outside, and we find that we are not only prayed in, but actually lived in – a model which, allowing for the limitations inherent in any use of models, seems more faithfully and creatively to reflect both our understanding of prayer and our experience of the act of praying. This understanding and experience are captured, all the more powerfully by coming, surely, from personal experience, by Alister McGrath:

> As they [Christians] kneel down to say their prayers, they are aware that in some way (which is very difficult to express in words) God is actually prompting them to pray. It is almost as if God is at work within them, creating a desire to pray, or to turn to God in worship and adoration. Yet God is also the one to whom they are praying. A similar situation arises in

worship. Although it is God whom we are praising, we are aware that it is somehow God himself who moves us from within to praise him.[12]

In this chapter, then, we have sought to draw together the often disparate realms of theology and prayer, and to indicate at least some of the ways in which the one is informed by the other. Theology and private prayer are not such distant relatives after all. Finally, we may wonder whether what would appear to be a widespread decline in the practice of private prayer – even among churchgoers – is not directly attributable to a failure as yet to replace one theological framework for it with another. That is, there is a feeling that the old framework (of prayer as being primarily our prayer addressed to a highly interventionist God, who confusingly and depressingly didn't seem actually to intervene very often) doesn't work any more – if indeed it ever did – and that for many people there is nothing to replace it with: a problem which is fed directly by our insistence on using the old framework as though it does work in public worship. We therefore need to articulate a new framework and re-integrate theology and private prayer once more so that theology can again inform our prayer and help us to understand what we are doing when we pray and so deepen and enrich our relationship with God. The potential for making these connections is there: they simply need to be made more clearly, more often, and more accessibly. If this happens then it may be, perhaps somewhat ironically, that it is the supposedly 'dry' study of theology which can become the means of infusing new life into our prayer and so lead us nearer to the heart of God – who is, after all, the reality at the centre both of our prayer and of our theology.

CHAPTER FOUR

Theology and Christian Practice

In the preceding two chapters we have examined some of the ways in which theology impinges upon (or should impinge upon) our prayer, both public and private. These prayers, if they are to be meaningful, must be at one level or another closely related to our daily life, a theme which Linda Woodhead elaborates with particular clarity in an essay in *New Soundings*:

> … rather than concentrating upon the cultivation of one's spiritual self and the spiritual sphere, Christian worship has generally been thought of as inseparably bound up with ethical action. The Christian sees the good life as a life in which love of self, God and neighbour are inseparably bound up with one another. The good life cannot therefore be confined to a private spiritual sphere, but will necessarily involve the public world, the world which God has made, a world worthy of love and care in all its parts and in all its concrete particularity.[1]

Given this relationship between prayer, worship and daily living, it is hardly surprising that the theological framework of Christianity should have substantial implications for Christian practice, just as it does for the life of prayer and worship. Theology, as Alister McGrath has already reminded us, is the ultimate source of Christian values, and therefore, in theory at least, the foundation of how we actually live our lives.[2]

This is certainly true in theory, but just as with prayer, I would be most surprised if the majority of 'ordinary Christians' have ever made – or even been encouraged to make – any overt connections between theology and life, and this may well go a long way towards explaining not only what McGrath calls the 'moral shallowness of Christian liberalism in recent years', but also a more general lack of ethical passion and urgency on the part of the bulk of the church. Certainly we have had our occasional prophets reminding us powerfully of the importance of this or that issue, but there is hardly a widespread sense in the church that the gospel which it lives is at least as important as the gospel which it professes to believe. This suggests that the connections between theology and the Christian life need to be made more explicit, and that new (or at least re-stated) connections need to be made, and made in a way which is accessible not merely to the professionally committed, but to the vast majority of parish church and local congregation based believers. Good theology need not, I continue to hope and pray, be abstruse theology also.

If a model is needed for the value of such a persistent effort to unite theology and the Christian life, it may perhaps be found pre-eminently in the letters of St Paul. This is not to say that one would necessarily wish to echo either all of St Paul's theological statements or his prescriptions for what constitutes Christian living. In two thousand years much has undoubtedly changed in our way of viewing both theology and ethics. What is important about St Paul, however, is his consistent method of yoking the two things together and recognising – and making plain also to his readers – that the one is influenced powerfully by the other. A perfect example of this method is to be found in the first two chapters of his Epistle to the Philippians, the centre-piece of which is the so-called Song of Christ's Glory. In these two chapters St Paul is exhorting his readers to a particular way of life, and doing so firmly within the highly theological context of the life, death and resurrection of Jesus Christ himself, and the indwelling of the Holy Spirit. The church at Philippi is to live in a certain way precisely because it believes certain things. For St Paul, theology and Christian practice are merely two sides of the same coin, two expressions of the one reality: our faith in God and our life for God.

St Paul's letters are occasional pieces, and he makes no effort to be comprehensive in his treatment even of those aspects of theology or practice which he identifies as significant. He is not so much concerned to be exhaustive as to set down certain initial guidelines upon which others may then build thereafter. Without wishing to draw any comparisons, a similar plea may be made for the present study. It would take what might be termed an 'applied systematics' to do full justice to the interrelationship between theology and Christian practice: it is only to be hoped that even a more piecemeal treatment in the wider context of this study may inspire or goad others to investigate the area more thoroughly and delineate it more clearly.

The present study, then, is not intended to represent a detailed topographical survey of the territory involved, but even on a more sweeping perusal of the terrain, certain landmarks emerge. The idea of Christian practice involves consideration of the way in which we live our lives and the use we make of them, and a logical starting-point is therefore the simple fact of our existence (and indeed of the existence of anything at all) and how we understand and interpret this theologically. This leads us to the Christian doctrine of creation, perhaps one of the least emphasised and – thanks to the battering which anything remotely connected with natural theology has received in recent generations – one of the least regarded of Christian doctrines. It is doubtful whether for most believers – even thoughtful ones – this doctrine receives anything more than a passing acknowledgement and a recognition that, 'Oh yes, God created the world', from which we can then pass on to the more pressing matters of salvation and eternity. To pass over the doctrine of creation in this way is, however, to ignore some profound theological pointers with regard to the nature of our life and an appropriate attitude and response towards it.

To begin with, the mere existence of a doctrine of creation (however one then proceeds to interpret it) is in itself a powerful statement of intent towards the universe and our life within it. The idea of creation immediately excludes the possibility that the universe (and therefore we ourselves) are an accident, and imbues all further thought and discussion with an element both of meaning and teleology. Life, if it is created (and therefore in some sense willed and purposive) has an inherent gravitas: it has from the outset a moral and spiritual significance built into it.

From this initial predisposition towards meaning and purpose, then, flow all of the other attitudes towards life which may be deduced from a specifically Christian doctrine of creation. Of these other attitudes, the first is one whose implications are – like the doctrine of creation itself – frequently overlooked. This is the simple fact that life, if it is not an accident, and is not (as it patently is not) self-caused, is a gift, and a gift which is, furthermore, lived always in the presence of the giver. This fact alone suggests certain responses to life. Of these, the pre-eminent one is gratitude. There is a richness, a potential, an incalculable *frisson* of excitement about the mere fact of being alive which it would be churlish to deny. This is not to claim, naïvely, that our experience of this gift of life is always perfect. Even the most fortunate of individuals will know at least moments of frustration, pain or loss, and one does not have to be acquainted with the world for very long to realise that life, for a great many people, contains, whether by accident or the inhumanity of others, a great deal more of pain than of pleasure. Our gratitude for our life with all of its potential, then, is necessarily tempered by our sorrow – or even our anger – at those aspects of it which, whether for others or for ourselves, have become disfigured by pain of whatever sort. And our gratitude itself is not thereby diminished: it is rather that our relationship with the giver is of such an intimate nature that we can share with him our sorrow and our anger in the knowledge that they are his also. Like the Psalmist, our heartfelt gratitude and our deepest pain go hand in hand, and both may be brought together to the God who created us capable of feeling them.

The presence of this 'existential' pain alongside our gratitude points the way to another facet of our response to life: that we are created to care for life (our own, others, the totality of the universe) and to exercise certain responsibilities with regard to it. If we sense – and share with God – our dismay at lives and circumstances which are marred by pain or anguish, then equally we feel ourselves moved (in our better moments at least) to attempt to redress the balance, to ease the lot of others in whatever ways we can, whether great or small. Such an inclination is, of course, then later reinforced, directed and to a greater or lesser extent codified both by our moral precepts and our society's laws and ethos, but I venture to suggest that the basic sense of responsibility towards the totality of our environment and its inhabitants is a part of our fundamental response to life, however misdirected or muddied that response may at times become.

Thirdly then, and equally 'instinctive' – although it is given additional credence by our sense of the value of life and the need to protect and enhance it, to which we have just alluded – is the conviction that human life, and indeed the whole of creation, is at bottom 'good'. It (and we) may be flawed, but these flaws, though they may obscure, do not extinguish the intrinsic 'goodness' of being or its capacity to reflect divinity. Matter, contrary to what many gnostic sects and sometimes even portions of mainstream Christianity (to all appearances, at least) have proclaimed, is not essentially 'evil', nor is it something which we must endure as best we can while waiting to be redeemed or released from it. Matter, no less than spirit, though doubtless in a different way, is good and is to be rejoiced in, as we are pointedly reminded in the creation myth in Genesis in which its creator rejoices in this same essential goodness: 'And God saw that it was good.' Or, as C. S. Lewis succinctly put it in, I think, *Mere Christianity*, 'God likes matter. He created it.'

To emphasise the importance of creation (both in general and in terms of the gift of our own unique human life) and our response to it is in no way to downplay the significance of a more salvation-oriented theology. It is merely to suggest that salvation should not be allowed to marginalise creation as it has so frequently threatened to do. That it might tend to do so is hardly surprising in a religion which places as much stress on revelation and the redeeming acts of God as Christianity does. Jesus Christ and the redemption which he wrought on the cross is the dominating central theme of the Christian faith, and the fact of that redemption and its necessity has an almost inevitable tendency to overshadow everything else, leading sometimes to a stiflingly heavy emphasis on human frailty, sin and guilt, and obscuring, or at least blurring, any image of goodness in our creation. Yes, we stand in need of redemption and forgiveness, but we need to be reminded also of the innate 'goodness' of all that is – ourselves included – and it is a reminder which has significant implications for our whole life of faith, for it conditions (as was remarked earlier in our discussion of prayer), our whole understanding of our relationship with God. We stand in need of redemption and forgiveness not as an essentially evil and depraved part of a doomed creation, but as beings whose essential goodness and likeness to God has become flawed and disfigured by evil, but who, with the creation itself, are ultimately destined to find (at once again and for the first time) the goodness to which we owe our being, and in the likeness of which, in the meantime, we ever strive to live.

These three reflections springing from the doctrine of creation (that life is a gift, that it carries with it responsibilities, and that it is intrinsically good) provide a starting point for the examination of the place of theology in Christian practice. Even by itself the doctrine of creation provides a general attitudinal framework towards our life and towards the whole of creation. But if our existence (and that of the rest of creation) evokes at least the beginning of an outlook on life, then the existence of God (and therefore the doctrine of God) fleshes out this general attitude substantially, and it is therefore to God and to the implications of his existence that we must now address our attention.

Certain aspects of the nature of God and his activity have been touched upon already, both in this chapter and in the discussion of prayer, and a number of other facets will be examined in due course, particularly the doctrine of the Incarnation. Here, though, I wish to concentrate not so much on any especial characteristics of God's identity or activity, but rather on the mere fact of his existence – or more correctly, I suppose, on the mere fact of our belief in his existence.

For belief in the existence of God – and certainly of God as he is conceived within the Christian tradition – carries with it immense significance for our understanding of ourselves and indeed for every part of our practical daily living. Whatever else we may want to say in the light of more specific considerations, the mere fact of belief in God's existence assumes some sort of acknowledgement that our life is lived under God or in the sight of God, and that we are both responsible and accountable to him for the use or abuse of that life – an understanding which mirrors that sense of responsibility which we identified as springing from our perception of ourselves as created beings.

This sense of a life lived in the sight of God also places our lives in the context of eternity, and thus once again a certain gravitas is imparted to our actions. What we do is not merely of transient significance, although that by itself may be substantial, but is rather part of a never-ending pattern of events, consequences and meanings which impinge not only on this world but on the next. Actions performed now may have, either for ourselves or for others, implications and reverberations into eternity.

The existence of God and the presence of an eternal perspective on our life imbues that life in its totality with what we might call a 'sacredness' so that there is (as we shall also see in the discussion of the Incarnation) no distinction to be made between supposedly sacred and secular parts of our life. The distinction is not, ontologically speaking, a valid one. As lived under God and within eternity all of our life is equally sacred. This is a vision which Christianity has by turns embraced and lost sight of, but at its best, as in, for example, the rich Celtic tradition of spirituality, there is a vibrant sense of the wholeness and interconnectedness – and indeed the sacredness – of every part of life and every action, however apparently humble, trivial or menial. There is no justification, therefore, for that kind of compartmentalising of life into sacred and secular (often with different standards) which Tom Lehrer satirised so astutely:

On Christmas day you can't get sore,
Your fellow-man you must adore:
There's time to rob him all the more
The other three-hundred-and-sixty-four!

Our life, if it is to reflect our faith adequately, must be, as it were, a seamless whole. Sunday churchgoing and office paper-clip pilfering are not compatible! As both the greatest prophets of the Old Testament and Jesus himself pointed out, religious observance and an ethical lifestyle must walk hand in hand, for only so can what we do bear adequate witness to what we believe. Theology, and indeed any specific doctrinal stance – even at the bare level of the existence of God – exercises a powerful influence on how we are to live.

If a belief merely in God's existence shapes our life and conditions our attitude towards it, then it is hardly surprising that his nature and his acts should impinge upon our understanding of our life even more compellingly. The primary consideration here is that of God's will and purpose for his creation – or at least our perception, however inadequate it may turn out to be, of that will. As revealed in scripture, and pre-eminently in Jesus Christ, that will is one of redemption – the transforming and renewing of all that is flawed or marred by evil or decay, such that in St Paul's words, 'the mortal must put on the immortal, and the perishable must put on the imperishable' and the creation, thus renewed, will at last reflect the perfect image and will of its creator.

The 'story' of our perception of God's will for his creation is an interesting and instructive one, in that it illustrates precisely how theology and practice are related – how what we believe about God shapes our values and indeed our specific actions arising from those values. It is perhaps a dangerous thing for a non-specialist to trespass on the territory of the biblical scholar, but regardless of the precise details of any particular formulation of the theory, it would appear to be the case that the Old

Testament reflects a variety of stages in a community's develop-
ing ideas about God, and at each stage what is believed about
God colours not only the life of any individual but also the life
(and often the 'political policy') of the nation.

Broadly speaking the perception of God would appear to
have moved from being initially that of a tribal God intimately
connected with particular places, to being then the God of a people ('the God of Abraham, Isaac and Jacob'), and then to being
the only God who created all things (hence the creation narra-
tives) but who had a unique covenant relationship with the people of Israel.

At this stage the effects of these beliefs are such as to cement
a people into a nation; to set them apart and to give them a
favoured status *vis-à-vis* other nations or tribes. This may merely
take the form of the repudiation of their gods or customs, or at
its most extreme, it may result in the wholesale destruction of
other peoples with full confidence in the approval of the deity –
who indeed is seen as requiring and then commanding the fight.

It is a tribute to the greatness of spirit of, for example, the
prophetic tradition, that the Jewish consciousness did not remain forever in this limited – but apparently very comfortable
position of assumed superiority and religious privilege. Doubtless the events of history, and in particular the experience of de-
feat, destruction and exile, helped to shatter any incipient com-
placency, but these events too required further interpretation
and a more profound questioning of the purposes of God which,
in large measure, the great prophets provided.

Two examples may perhaps illustrate the depth of soul-
searching and the measure of change in religious outlook and
world view which was involved. Thus the figure known as
deutero-Isaiah takes the unprecedented step of pointing to a foreign ruler, Cyrus, as the Lord's anointed, his instrument and the
one who will achieve his purposes. Admittedly these purposes
are directly connected with the restoration and rehabilitation of
the people of Israel, so the invocation of Cyrus is not without
self-interest, but whatever the motives involved, deutero-Isaiah's

previously undreamed-of boldness marks a quantum leap in the theological understanding of God. God may still have a special relationship with his chosen people through his covenant with them, but he is now presented as the God of all people, whether or not they recognise or acknowledge him, and he is therefore revealed as a God who may have what relationship he chooses with any or all people. The Jewish people may be special to God, but the possibility is opened up that all people may be special to God and not merely the Jews.

Similarly, during the exile, Ezekiel counsels the exiled Jews to pray for the prosperity of Babylon. At one level this might also smack of self-interest and may be ascribed to simple pragmatism – Ezekiel is astute enough to realise (and to make it plain to his readers also) that the prosperity of the Jews who live there is directly related to that of Babylon itself. At another level, however, Ezekiel is being every bit as radical theologically as deutero-Isaiah, because the implication is that other peoples and nations stand in need of prayer, can justifiably be the objects of prayer, and that God can and will respond to prayers on their behalf, suggesting that he has their welfare at heart just as he has the welfare of the Jewish people at heart – a position which is also reinforced within the prophetic tradition by the story of Jonah and God's concern for the people of Nineveh.

Alongside these two developments, and evinced especially in some of the minor prophets, runs the growing and increasingly clearly articulated conviction that religious practice and ritual are not enough, and that God is at least as much interested in social justice and integrity of personal life as he is in the observance of religious times and seasons. Here again the strict formalism of a legalistic religious framework is beginning to stretch and crack open under the pressure of a larger spirit within.

From a Christian perspective, this process of re-envisioning the purposes of God in ever larger terms at once gathered pace and was definitively expressed in the person of Jesus Christ. He it was who completed the fracturing of any form of legalistic religiosity which had been begun by the prophets. He quite clearly

placed so-called religious laws second to the paramount consideration of duty, charity or need; he reminded his followers of the
prior necessity of reconciliation with one's neighbour before approaching God, and he made the same pattern apply in terms of
forgiveness in the model prayer which he taught them; and he
was outspoken in his criticism of the religious establishment and
its hollow legalism in such passages as the parable of the
Pharisee and the publican at prayer. For Jesus, even more acutely
than for the prophets, our religious life is not separable from the
rest of our life. As we touched on earlier in this discussion, quite
simply the two things are one, and our understanding of our religious practice and our theology have to expand to meet the
new vision.

It is the same when we turn to the position of Jesus with regard to God's will for the redemption of his creation. Here too
Jesus builds on all that has gone before – on the breadth of vision
of such prophets as deutero-Isaiah and Ezekiel – but again Jesus
goes beyond them and inaugurates a new dimension and vision
which Christian theology and doctrine have ever afterwards
been challenged to assimilate. For in the person of Jesus we see
revealed the full breadth of God's compassion, which embraces
even – and perhaps especially – the frailest and weakest and the
most unlikely and apparently unpromising parts of his creation.
Sometimes it is salutary and startling to be reminded of this fact:

> than his open attitude towards the poor, the weak, the sick
> and the despised. He eats with sinners, includes prostitutes
> in his fellowship, goes home with tax collectors, and displays
> an unprecedented spirit of equality towards women.[3]

Possibly the most obvious and immediately striking of the evid-
ences of this compassion is to be found in Jesus' ministry of healing. All who seek healing at Jesus' hands find it there, and none
is turned away. And significantly, among them are many who
are in one way or another 'beyond the pale': the unclean such as
lepers and the woman with the flow of blood; the Gentile as well
as the Jew, such as the Syro-Phoenician woman's daughter. But

the breadth of this divine compassion and will for wholeness is not confined merely to embracing all people – which would be a somewhat external measure of its breadth, though remarkable enough in itself – but is expressed also in a will towards perfect wholeness which embraces both body and soul. I make no claim to particular expertise in the niceties of biblical exegesis (especially when it comes to Greek etymology!), but it would certainly appear that there are occasions on which the gospel writers depict Jesus as being concerned with the whole person rather than merely with the body. In the case of the paralytic lowered through the roof (Mark 2:1-12) there is a clear link between the physical and the spiritual when Jesus says: 'Which is easier: to say to the paralytic, "Your sins are forgiven" or to say, "Get up, take up your mat and walk".' Similarly, there is presumably an intended distinction to be drawn (since a different word is deliberately used in each case) in the cleansing of the ten lepers (Luke 17:11-19) between the nine who were merely cleansed and the tenth, whose faith has made him 'well' or 'whole'. That this distinction, and the concern of Jesus with the healing of both body and soul is intentional is reinforced in a different context by the deliberate parallelism between the accounts of the feeding of the five thousand and the feeding of the four thousand. In the first of these two accounts (Mark 6:30-44) Jesus has compassion on the crowd because they are 'like sheep without a shepherd', and in the second (Mark 8:1-13) his compassion is aroused because 'they have already been with me three days and have nothing to eat'. The compassion of God in Christ embraces both soul and body.

But Jesus' compassion is displayed not merely in his response to direct need – whether physical or spiritual – but more generally, and perhaps more profoundly, in his response to people 'as they are' and in his appreciation of the intrinsic value of even the most despised and rejected of outcasts, often, indeed, at the expense of the more apparently 'acceptable' members of society. Such an attitude is displayed in parables: the pharisee and the publican, and the parable of the Good Samaritan spring im-

mediately to mind; in Jesus' willingness to eat with 'tax collec-
tors and sinners' and to befriend the most unpromising of individuals such as Zaccheus (not to mention the apostles!); and it is
spelt out in detail in one or two 'set pieces', among which the
episode in the house of Simon the Pharisee (Luke 7:36-50) is
probably the most pointed, especially as it appears to be a deliberate re-working and variation by the author of St Luke's gospel
on the anointing of Jesus at the house of Simon the Leper (Mark
14:1-9). In the eyes of Luke's Simon, the woman is a 'sinner',
someone with whom Jesus should have no dealings. For Jesus,
though, whatever the woman may have done until this moment,
there is an abiding worth and value in her present expression of
contrition through tears, and in her acts of service and homage
to Jesus himself – acts which, Jesus gently but incisively reminds
Simon, Simon has himself neglected. In a very real sense the
woman is 'redeemed' and rehabilitated by the value which Jesus
attributes to her sorrow and simple devotion, such that he can
say to her at the end of the episode, 'Your faith has saved you; go
in peace.' Her sins are not glossed over, but are overtly forgiven
and the woman is reassured that her love places her within the
range of God's love: she gives her love and is thus enabled to receive the gift of God's love and with it his forgiveness. As much
as any of the crippled or the lepers, this woman is healed by her
encounter with Jesus.

Less dramatic in our eyes, but probably equally startling at the
time, is the respect and affection with which Jesus treated those
who were not outcasts perhaps, but who were certainly undervalued and underprivileged in their society. When the disciples try
to restrain the children from coming to Jesus he rebukes them,
and indeed does not merely allow the children to come to him but
even finds in them the qualities of the kingdom of heaven: far
from keeping them at a distance, the disciples are actually to learn
from the children and become like them. Likewise the value in the
eyes of God of these apparently insignificant children is reinforced by Jesus' teaching on the wrath which will be poured out
on those who cause any of 'these my little ones' to sin.

Like children, women too were granted a new dignity and worth by Jesus. Women figure prominently in the gospel stories, and as many recent writers (following the re-discovery of the fact by early feminist theologians) have commented, they occupy a position of particular privilege in the gospels. Jesus is recorded as speaking to women in situations where this would not be the norm, such as the Samaritan woman at the well in chapter four of St John's gospel; he is recorded as being tended and ministered to by a group of women; he numbers women such as Martha and Mary among his especial friends; and it is women who take upon themselves the burdensome and distressing duty of watching and grieving at the crucifixion. Finally, and most significantly, it is women who witness the first resurrection appearances of Jesus, and who are commissioned by Jesus with the first proclamation of the gospel – to go and tell the other disciples; and it is, of course, with a glorious irony, men who will, initially at least, not believe them, but dismiss it as an 'idle tale'.

In Jesus then, we see brought to fulfilment what had been hinted at and glimpsed in the greatest of the Israelite prophets – the all-embracing nature of the divine love and of the divine will for the healing and ultimate wholeness of all that had been created: a will which finds an almost poetic echo in St Paul's meditation on the redeeming work of Christ and the indwelling of the Holy Spirit in Romans chapter eight. This will, as seen in action in Jesus, is characterised by the embracing of all who seek, however tentatively and with whatever misgiving or failings, to place themselves within its ambit, and by the presence of a constantly offered forgiveness for these very failings, a forgiveness which only needs to be accepted to be effectual as an experienced reality. It is hardly surprising that Jesus told the parable of the Prodigal Son, or that it has come to be so often seen as a paradigm of the open arms and fixed will for the good of his erring children of God himself. God's will for his creation, as foreshadowed in the prophets, and made manifest in Jesus Christ – in his life and pre-eminently in his death – is for the redemption of that creation expressed in a passionate reaching out towards it, and once again this must have monumental consequences for our understanding of our life, its purpose and our attitude towards it, especially when it is linked, as it must be, with the central doctrine of the Incarnation to which some attention must therefore now be paid.

Thus far we have considered a variety of the things that Jesus said and did, and what these reveal or suggest about the will of God. However, it is inevitable that any such analysis of the ministry of Jesus leads directly to the question of what or who he was, and therefore, within the framework of Christianity to the doctrine of the Incarnation.

This study is not intended to be – or even to include – a fully worked-out christology, and I am not concerned here with the finer points of christological or incarnational doctrine or with the minutiae of the very real problem of how to translate the categories of Greek metaphysics into contemporary thought forms. This is in no way to deny that these activities are vital. They are, and they have been explored in exemplary depth and with a passionate conviction of this importance by many scholars, perhaps especially John Macquarrie, whose sense of urgency is evinced by the fact that his monumental work, *Jesus Christ in Modern Thought*, has not prevented him from declaring, only a few years later, that christology must be 'revisited'. It does matter that we should understand as well as we are able just how it is possible for the human and divine to co-exist in one individual, and how (whether expressed in metaphysical, psychological or any other terms) the nature of such an individual may be most convincingly portrayed. However, the performance of this task is only one aspect of the totality of what needs to be done, and if done in isolation it merely accentuates rather than diminishes the gap between theology and daily Christian living to which we have consistently made reference. For it is quite conceivable that one might 'construct' – if that is an appropriate description of the activity – a thoroughly praiseworthy and convincing account of how the Incarnation is to be understood which answers all of the most awkward metaphysical questions adequately (or even, on an intellectual level, inspiringly) and yet entirely fail to connect this abstract being with the more mundane realities of the church in the here and now. When this happens – as it has sometimes happened – the child of the Incarnation is still-born.

The other, and equally vital part of the task of any theology of the Incarnation is to make plain at least some of the ways in which – and regardless of precise metaphysical formulations – the concept of Incarnation impinges upon us and contributes still further to the shaping of what we have characterised here as our 'response to life'. In other words, what does an Incarnational faith imply, or even dictate, about our way of looking at our life and of living it both individually and corporately?

Here I wish merely to suggest four areas in which a doctrine of the Incarnation contributes towards the formulation of our identity and purpose as Christians, and which together lead directly into a consideration of how we understand ourselves communally, that is, as the church. The doctrine of the Incarnation shades almost imperceptibly into ecclesiology, our doctrine of the church.

First then, the Incarnation enables us to see how in a human life – albeit admittedly a divine one also – the divine will, which we have characterised as being a will towards redemption and wholeness, is 'cashed out'. The theoretical possibilities are almost endless, and any one of them, were it to have become a reality, would have implied certain things about our own lives as followers of the God of the Incarnation.

Thus it would appear, for example, that some, at least, of Jesus' followers had a particular set of ideas in mind regarding the role and nature of the Messiah. He was to be the 'warrior king', the one to set them free from the hated oppression of foreign rule, a figure of strength and of majesty, and had Jesus indeed been a Messiah in this mould it might well have been that his followers down the ages would have made this supposed

strength and power a model, and that the church might have become a kind of latter-day reflection of the Maccabees.

In the event, however, Jesus turned out not to be a divine
'strong-arm' figure, but a very different kind of Messiah. Far
from being revealed in a show of divine strength, the ultimate
reality of the divine nature is shown in Jesus to be one of self-
giving and self-offering without limit. What Jesus did reveals for
an Incarnational faith who God is, and it is immediately significant therefore that even the earliest Christian communities and
the earliest extant Christian writer, St Paul, saw in Jesus a pattern for Christian living. To the reader of the New Testament
one of the most striking features of the early Christian communities is their emphasis on service, expressed through such
things as the appointment of deacons and St Paul's concern with
the support by the other churches of the Christian community in
Jerusalem. For St Paul, and for the whole of the early Church, if
it is to reflect the divine will for redemption and wholeness as
this has been expressed in Jesus, the Christian life must be likewise one of self-giving, of 'forbearance' and forgiveness, of, if
necessary, being martyred with (like Stephen) words of forgiveness on our lips. As a way of living it is not merely a tall order
but a counsel of perfection, but for St Paul, as for Jesus himself,
as God is, so we also must seek to be.

In the Incarnation, then, we are offered a basic pattern of life
and it is one which is not merely human, but is divine also: our
life is, essentially, an exercise in *imitatio Dei*, and this leads us
necessarily to the second of the areas in which an Incarnational
faith shapes the most basic foundations both of our attitudinal and
practical response to life. It is almost inevitable that any theistic
faith – or at least any which sees God or the gods as 'good' – will
have within it some intimation of the need to become 'god-like'
or to seek union with the god or gods. But this has the potential
to be a barren and depressing business in a non-incarnational
faith. If it is up to us, as human beings, to become god-like, then
there arises the question of how the gulf between the human and
the divine, the creator and the created, the eternal and the tem-

poral, the good and (at best) the not-so-good, can possibly be bridged. And furthermore there is not necessarily any indication from the divine perspective of how this bridge can be made, except through our own efforts, which, from humbling and bitter experience, we know to be doomed to failure.

The doctrine of the Incarnation changes this somewhat gloomy scenario radically and for ever. Through it human nature is shown, and not by means of any inherent quality, but rather through the power of God, to have the potential – if it is not blasphemous to say so – of encompassing divinity. All the frailties and failings of that same human nature are not sufficient to prevent God from claiming it as his own, transforming and renewing it, and through it showing forth his nature, revealed as we have sketched above, in gracious and compassionate self-giving. It is at this point, of course, that the apparent abstractions of metaphysical thinking about the Incarnation come most properly into prominence, for if the above remarks are to be remotely credible there needs to be some clearly thought out understanding of just how it might be possible for the human and the divine to co-exist equally, separately and yet indivisibly, within the compass of one individual human life, that of Jesus Christ. Indeed, given this requirement, one can see why the early Fathers grew so passionate in their theological disputes, for as we have noted already, the smallest change in doctrinal formulation will have an immediate influence on what can or cannot be assumed or believed about the will and/or the activity of God. How we understand him theologically will provide logical limits as to how we may interpret his will and actions.

Assuming, however, that such a cogent christology can be worked out and expressed in meaningful contemporary categories of thought, the idea of human nature being able, as we have expressed it, to encompass divinity, becomes a reality. It must be admitted at this point that there is here an issue to be resolved *vis-à-vis* the status of 'holiness' or 'goodness' within other, and especially non-incarnational, religions. It would be foolish and arrogant to deny that such goodness and holiness

exist, or indeed that they have sometimes shone more brightly
elsewhere than within Christianity. However, from a Christian
perspective this goodness must be seen – if it is not being a religious imperialist to say so – as being the result of a divine indwelling of the kind which we have outlined here. Without such
an indwelling, human nature is not capable of such an *imitatio
Dei* and it is the Incarnation which provides us, as Christians,
with our foundational pattern for understanding this indwelling.

That said, the effects of this indwelling of God through the
Holy Spirit – hence the close links between christology and trinitarian theology – have been, and still are today, plainly to be
seen in many Christian lives, and such goodness and holiness
when we experience them speak plainly to us of the presence of
Christ through the Holy Spirit and of the nature of God himself.
A child was once asked the question: 'What is a saint?' and,
thinking of the figure she had seen in the stained-glass windows
in her local parish church answered unhesitatingly, 'Someone
the light shines through.' After all the attempts of the wise and
the learned to identify the nature of sanctity, 'out of the mouths
of babes and sucklings …'! For the people we perceive as saintly
are precisely those whom the light shines through, the light of
God himself, given by God himself and merely radiated in self-
giving love by those who are 'transparent' enough to allow the
light to pierce through without becoming obscured by the darkness of the self.

What is true of our imaging of God in our lives is true also of
our goal – or more correctly our hope – of union with God: the
possibility of this union being something which the Eastern
Orthodox churches especially have emphasised through their
use of the concept of 'deification' as a part of the process of salvation. This Orthodox insight is valuable, for within an
Incarnational framework of belief this hope too is genuinely
made accessible to us, and for precisely the same reason that a
genuine *imitatio Dei* becomes a possibility, namely that it depends primarily not upon our own effort but upon the power

and the love of the God who calls us to himself. Attainment of union with God is not even dependent upon our 'success' in growing into his likeness, but depends, on our part, only upon our desire to be with him, a desire which is perfectly compatible with the continuance of all our human frailty and fallibility as St Paul so eloquently demonstrates in Romans 7:15-25 – a passage which ends with precisely the affirmation of the power of God to do what human nature cannot do of which we have spoken here: 'Thanks be to God – through Jesus Christ our Lord!'

At this point christology overlaps to a certain extent with the doctrine of the Atonement, for it is the doctrine of the Atonement which proclaims the possibility of our union with God. Again here I do not propose to survey the various possible theories of the atonement, but merely to note that it is this doctrine which proclaims the breaking down of barriers and the possibility (and the reality) of reconciliation between us and God. Conversely, of course, atonement depends on christology, for the divinity and humanity of Jesus Christ need both to be adequately acknowledged and convincingly related if atonement is to be rendered credible.

Through the death and resurrection of Jesus Christ, then, the way is opened to union with God, and this union is then realised through the indwelling of the Holy Spirit and fostered through the sacramental and spiritual life of the church. At every stage of the way, both in this life and in what we conjecture or hope for in the world to come, the initiative is with God, exactly as we have argued that it is with prayer, so that there are echoes here of the idea of prayer as something which is done within us. Just so, our journey to (and with) God is something which is wrought in us, and is something which we need only to desire and accept in order for it to take place. An Incarnational faith inspires us with the hope (and the experiential knowledge) that the goals of faith are not dependent upon an impossible task such as our own pursuit of perfection, but upon the loving and redeeming work of the God who has both created us and then shared with us in the life of his creation.

These first two areas in which the doctrine of the Incarnation affects our response to life are primarily concerned with the shaping of our perceptions, our understanding of the divine will and the basic structure of our own alignment with that will. To a large extent the third and fourth areas complement this by offering us a discrete sense of how this will is to be lived out, both personally and corporately as the church. Thus the third 'lantern for our path' which the Incarnation provides is the integration of the sacred and the secular, to which we have already made some reference above. All religions have had their sacred places and sacred times, and usually these are sharply to be distinguished from more secular times and places. Within Judaism – and Islam also – as forms of what has come to be called ethical mono-theism, there is a tension in the relationship between the two realms in that sometimes there appears to be a sharp disjunction between them and at other times the distinctions between them collapse. Thus holy places abound – the Temple, the ground around the burning bush and so on – but equally the prophets often equate holiness and God's will with social justice and com-passion and place these things before more apparently 'reli-gious' duties and rituals.

Finally, in the Incarnation (though, it has to be said, not al-ways within the life of the religion founded on that Incarnation) the sacred and the secular are seen to occupy the same space and time, for not only are all places and times created by God, but God has himself dwelt within the apparently secular human realm and sacralised the whole of human life. It is not so much that sacred and secular have merged, as that all has become sacred. The result of this is that 'religion', 'spirituality', 'the will of God' and so on are no longer distant, other-worldly or es-capist notions – if indeed they ever were. Rather, they are to do with the here and now as much as with the hereafter; they are to do with the 'real world'; with joy and pain; with our neighbour and with our enemy; with our family and with our community; with our society and with our environment. God, through the Incarnation (both by the simple fact of it, and by the specific teaching and actions of Jesus) is present in, and has a will for all of these human concerns. Indeed, they are the place in which God's will for his creation is most clearly manifested. We are reminded again of the fusion of prayer, theology and life, a fusion which is most felicitously encapsulated in the closing words of many modern language services of the eucharist: 'Go in peace to love and serve the Lord. In the name of Christ. Amen.' Worship and life, sacred and secular are, through God in Christ, all of a piece.

The fourth and final area identified here in which the Incarnation shapes our response to life and our understanding of ourselves is in its bestowal of an identity and a commission both upon the individual believer and upon the church. This identity and commission are, of course, co-extensive: the commission provides the identity, and the identity (in so far as it is successfully assumed) signifies in turn the fulfilment of the commission. Thus in the wake of the Incarnation the church is to be, through the Holy Spirit, Christ's continuing presence on earth and, in a very real sense, a continuation of the Incarnation, an identity which was appropriated very early on in the life of the church, being reflected in St Paul's image of the church as the Body of Christ and the individual believer as a member of that Body. As a commission this is derived from a variety of sources, not merely the so-called 'Great Commission' in Matthew twenty-eight. Other sources would include a number of passages from St John's gospel: 'I have called you', 'As the Father sent me, so I send you' and so on. But whichever passages of scripture one appeals to, the end result is that which is so beautifully expressed by St Teresa of Avila in her familiar meditation:

> Christ has now no body on earth but yours,
> No hands but yours, no feet but yours;
> Yours are the eyes through which must look out
> Christ's compassion on the world.
> Yours are the feet with which
> He is to go about doing good.
> Yours are the hands with which
> He is to bless people now.

It is at this point that, as we remarked earlier, Incarnation and christology shade almost imperceptibly into ecclesiology. For in this Incarnation-derived commission is the essence both of the church's self-understanding and of its practical task. It dictates – doubtless amongst many other things – two aspects in particular of that task: first, that the Church's mission is an inclusive rather than an exclusive one, and secondly that, to use an appropriate piece of jargon, the church is a 'hands-on' organisation.

The church is to be inclusive as it seeks to live out the life of Christ, who, as commented earlier, received all who would come to him: if this, as revealed in Jesus Christ, is the nature of God and the breadth of his love, then the church has no mandate to place anyone outside the scope of that love. Similarly, the church must be 'hands-on' in the sense in which Archbishop George Carey described it as being the 'church in the market place'. Any ecclesiology which sees the church as being in any sense a 'holy huddle' or which threatens to separate the life of the church from the life of the world is clearly suspect. Furthermore, this requirement of inclusiveness and involvement with the life of the world must surely exercise an influence on our personal lifestyle, and on the church's 'social policy' and concern for outreach into the community.

As far as personal lifestyle is concerned, enough has been said already about the place of Jesus Christ as a pattern for our living to indicate at least some of the effects which Jesus' commission and the church's identity as the presence of Christ on earth should have. With regard to the church as a corporate entity, I wish briefly here to allude merely to two realms of inclusiveness and involvement which seem to be to be essential if the church is to fulfil its commission and assume its true identity.

First, and once again following the example of Jesus, the church is bound to have an especial concern for those on the margins of society, those whom, in various ways, the 'market place' has left behind. This is easy to say and far harder to do, for it will never be easy for any congregation – who are always

going to be the ones at the 'coalface' of the church's endeavours
– to assimilate those with whom the rest of society may feel for
one reason or another uneasy: the unemployed; social misfits;
the alienated; AIDS victims; the excluded; the asylum seekers
and so on. But if the church is truly to be Christ-like – and if it is
not then it is hard to see how it can claim to be Christ's church –
then these groups and many others have to be held dear to it,
and both cared for and loved at a local and personal level and,
where necessary, lobbied for and supported on a wider canvas.

Secondly, the church – and specifically its theological thinking – needs to be involved with all of the major ethical issues of
the day: medical ethics, including embryology and fertilisation
techniques; abortion; euthanasia; genetic engineering and the
like. As Janet Martin Soskice has rightly commented,[4] ethics is at
the 'cutting edge' of the Christian faith, and it is essential that
the church's beliefs, theology and practice are related meaningfully to one another, such that in these areas as in others, what
we do is informed and shaped by the structure of what we believe.

In practice the church's record of manifesting this close connection between theology and life and enabling its life to be informed and renewed by its theology is somewhat patchy.
Certain individuals and periods stand out, such as St Paul and
the early church in general, but there have been many other periods
in which few, if any, connections appear to have been made between the beliefs of the church and the manner of its life.

In the present generation there has been a number of attempts to revitalise the connection, such as, in England, the Faith
in the City programme, and in South America the various forms
of liberation theology which have emerged, and in a wider geographical context, the substantial contributions of feminist theology and womanist theology in a number of areas. Valuable
though these efforts are, however, they are somewhat piecemeal, being targeted towards very specific situations and seeking equally specific and limited goals: they have not, in a wider
sense, resulted in a thoroughgoing reappraisal of the nature of

the church or its calling, nor of how its theological thinking provides a rationale, shape and direction to that calling.

Disturbingly also, there would appear to be a sense among many people, perhaps especially the young, and in spite of a wide-ranging and diffuse (if often ill-defined) spiritual hunger, and a good deal of idealism and altruism in that same group, that the church, in its more mainstream forms at least, is losing its way at present. If this observation is accurate, then it might well be argued that it is precisely in a lack of connection between theology and Christian practice that this lost direction consists. To many people the church appears to worship and conduct its own internal life in something of a vacuum, and it is hard for people outside it (and sometimes even for those inside it!) to see just what difference the church's professed beliefs actually make; how what the church preaches gives Janet Martin Soskice's 'cutting edge' to its actions. In the present discussion we have found that there are potentially many connections to be made between theology and Christian practice, and it would appear that if the church is to present a credible witness in the contemporary world, these connections must be meaningfully made in just the same way as they must be made between theology and other areas of Christian life, and what we believe and what we do must be, and be seen to be, in a relationship of complete mutuality.

CHAPTER FIVE

Theology and Dogmatism

In the course of the three previous chapters we have explored the need for connections to be made between theology and a number of areas of the church's life, and looked briefly at precisely what some of these connections might be and how these might influence the church's practice. Having done this, it is important at this stage to return to the central theme of the nature of the theological task itself in order to see in more detail how the task of forging and refining theology should be conducted. For it is all very well to suggest that theology should have a particular function within the life of the church, but this needs to be complemented by a clear sense of how this theology is formulated and in what manner of thinking it properly consists.

A useful starting-place is provided by the idea alluded to in Chapter One, that theology provides a 'space for belief'. This phrase perhaps requires some explanation. It is a phrase which is intended to convey the perception that the Christian faith is neither a prison nor a desert: it neither hems us in by denying us all freedom nor leaves us so free as to be directionless. Thus Christianity is unashamedly a historical faith with its roots both in the person of Jesus Christ and also stretching back into the ancient faith-history of the Jewish people. We have therefore a clearly defined historical tradition, but this is to be responded to not slavishly but creatively, and history must be allowed to interact with our present experience. So, for example, although we are firmly committed to a belief in the resurrection of Jesus Christ from the dead as an historical event, we are not thereby blindly committed to any one interpretation of this event or to the historicity of every word of the scriptural accounts of that resurrection. We may or may not wish to claim veracity for the sighting of angels or the rolling away of the stone or the eating of fish, but the historical reality of the resurrection (whatever we make of the particular scriptural accounts) will be reinforced and confirmed by our present experience of Christ as risen and active in our worship, prayer and daily living.

Similarly, just as we are rooted in, but not chained to history (and as our theology must reflect present as well as past experience), so too our theological framework provides a living space for our beliefs rather than shackles to tie them down. Again we are, for example, committed to a belief in the atoning death of Jesus Christ on the cross, but the doctrine of the atonement does not insist on any one model or interpretation of the exact means by which Christ's death achieves forgiveness, reconciliation and salvation. Such a firm yet flexible framework is potentially a major asset for Christianity, for it recognises our need for a measure of freedom in our perceptions and understanding, and yet it meets also a fundamental human need for pattern and order rather than the chaos of unlimited autonomy.

In the present chapter, then, this notion of theology as providing a 'space for belief' will be explored somewhat further, and we shall examine some of the consequences of such an understanding of theology for the manner in which it is to be undertaken, an examination which will, in turn, have substantial implications for the final two areas with which we are concerned in this study – the place of theology in ecumenical relationships, and the relationship of theology with the human psyche.

Having advocated this flexible approach, I am aware that there are many who would take exception to the idea of a 'space for belief' right from the start. For, I suspect, a substantial percentage of the church, both lay and ordained, theologian and non-theologian, theology has a rather more concrete and directly prescriptive function than I have allowed: it tells us what – and if possible exactly what – we are to believe. Its function is to protect the faith and the faithful, to exclude heresy, to reassure rather than to provoke questions, to engender, in so far as it is possible, a certainty in faith which is proof against whatever negative and corrosive influences may be perceived as lurking beyond its boundaries. According to this view – which admittedly may be held in less as well as more extreme forms – theology is there not so much to enable us to construct a flexible living space, but to erect a fortress for our safety with clearly defined notions as to who (and what ideas) are inside and outside its walls.

This, in turn, is a conception of theology which I would wish, and hardly surprisingly given all that has been said up to this point, vigorously to refute. I would wish to do so principally for three reasons, each of which is significant enough to deserve substantial attention here. First, then, any such an unswervingly positive and affirmative approach to theology is virtually bound almost entirely to neglect one of the fundamental axes of Christian theology: the *via negativa* or, as it is known in another of its guises, the apophatic tradition. Admittedly, as I have commented elsewhere,[1] this has received something of a battering during the present century at the hands of W. R. Inge and others, and in a climate which is often inimical to Christianity one can see why it should not prove to be universally popular as a theological method. In the face of any threat, certainty (however spurious) has a natural tendency to look more immediately attractive than any more tentative method or any acknowledgement of the limits of our understanding as far as the things of God are concerned.

Such a desire for theological comfort is, however, not a valid argument for the neglect of so central a part of the theological enterprise, for the *via negativa* is, as Aquinas rightly divined, a necessary preliminary to any more positive expression of our theology. Whatever else we may wish to go on to say positively about God, it is essential that we should first acknowledge the limits both of our understanding and of our language, neither of which is ultimately adequate to the task or capable of encapsulating – or even depicting – the God who is their object. More will be said at a later stage in the discussion, but our starting point must be that the creature can never, by definition, encompass its creator: our human understanding can never fully comprehend or express in human language the divine nature.

There is a subsidiary, although nonetheless equally vital, aspect to any neglect of the *via negativa*, which is the fact that such neglect tends also to diminish or ignore the spiritual legacy of the negative way of the great Christian mystics, and on a more mundane level, the experience of this same negative way in our own life of prayer. It is not for nothing that one of the great medieval classics of spirituality is entitled *The Cloud of Unknowing*, for this state of unknowing is one reached by all of the mystics, both ancient and modern. Similarly, I suspect, something like this experience, although possibly to a lesser degree, is common to most of us more ordinary Christians in the best of our praying at least. By this I mean that there comes a point at which we discover two things: that absolute cognitive knowledge concerning God is not, in fact, accessible to us, and secondly that this is not really the kind of knowledge which the spiritual life is about anyway. Insofar as we speak of having 'knowledge of God' what we actually mean by this is not abstract cognitive knowledge about some other entity than ourselves, but something much closer to what Michael Polanyi has called 'personal knowledge', a knowledge which is entirely compatible with our inability fully to encompass or express God. So an over-affirmative approach to theology neglects, then, not only a basic theological principle but also an equally basic reality of spiritual experience.

The second of the problems associated with an overly self-confident approach to theology lies precisely in its own certainty – a need for the absence of which we have argued earlier – for a significant consequence of a self-confidence which borders on arrogance is the pejorative effect which it has on the relationship of theology to other disciplines. At all points in its history, theology has had to face up to the task of reacting to the discoveries, theories and categories of other realms of thought, whether scientific (as for much of the nineteenth century), philosophicolinguistic (as for much of the twentieth century) or whatever. This task has perhaps never been as pressing or as vital both to theology itself and to the world beyond it as it is today. In the previous chapter we adverted to the requirement that theology should interact with the multifarious ethical and social issues of the day, and in the same way there is still a conversation to be carried on with, among others, the disciplines of science and philosophy – to say nothing of the arts. In this conversation an attitude such as we have been advocating in the present discussion is essential, for there will be occasions when theology will need to allow itself to be moulded (or even, in one aspect or another, entirely re-directed) by external stimulation, just as there will be occasions when theology will impinge upon the thinking of the scientist or the philosopher, as in the growing use of the category of 'faith' in relation to scientific knowledge. For theology to approach the discussion secure in the conviction of its own intrinsic and unshakeable 'rightness', regardless of what anyone may say to the contrary, may initially appear comfortable. In reality, however, it invalidates the discussion immediately, cutting theology off from any meaningful contact with the wider world of academic and speculative thought and thereby contributing substantially, and ultimately fatally, to its own perceived irrelevance to which reference has been made in the opening chapters of this study. The very certainty which once looked so attractive will have proved in the end to be the Trojan horse of theology, allowing in, under its cover, the mortal enemies of aridity and sterility.

If these first two objections to an over-confident way in theology are principally concerned with its 'academic' failings, then the third is, by contrast, purely pragmatic. It is simply that when translated into attitudes, opinions and lifestyle as far as church communities are concerned, the results of this strain of theology are all too often bordering on the arrogant and the self-opinionated, and are, as a result, unappealing in the extreme. And one does encounter church communities which are like this. Marked by rigidity and hemmed in by a conviction of divine command on every conceivable topic, they are unbending and closed to every position but their own – which, it goes without saying, is the 'right' one. In such communities it becomes very clear who is 'in' and who is 'out', and the pre-conditions for moving from one to the other are made equally plain. Alongside this conviction of intrinsic 'rightness' there runs, as an almost inevitable corollary, an equally strong conviction as to the 'wrongness' of others, and a judgemental attitude towards those whose opinions are different. Again, if this appears to be merely an abstract statement, I can only add that personal experience has confirmed the truth of it. Not once, but several times in the course of parochial ministry, have I been informed that I and many other Christians are 'not saved', and I have had frequent experience of churches refusing to participate in ecumenical events because this would mean associating with those who are 'not saved' and risking contamination thereby.

A final consequence of this kind of stance is that it has a tendency to lead (ironically, given that it is founded on an over-confident theology) to a faith which engenders fear rather than love, especially in its evangelistic techniques. To know who is 'in' and who is 'out' is very comfortable for those who are 'in', and it is, even today, potentially a very powerful evangelistic device to be able to assure those who are 'out' that hell is their ultimate destination unless they conform to the rules and come 'in'. It goes almost without saying, too, that the hell which is invoked in this way is a fully-blown medieval one complete with fiery lakes, demons and pitch forks! In this context too I have known a number of children who have returned from summer camps (or even single evening events) organised by such churches, and who have been genuinely deeply afraid, having been told that they and their parents (often sincere and devout members of my own congregation) are heading for hell unless they embrace whatever form of rigid fundamentalist Christianity the children have been exposed to. Such teaching appears to be at best sub-Christian, and it is the practical fruits of it which set the seal on my own mistrust of rigidity and over-certainty in theology. Both theologically and practically it is too narrow and too limiting in its effects adequately to reflect the mystery, the majesty and yet the humility of the divine love which is at the heart of our faith, or to acknowledge fully our human inadequacy as we attempt falteringly to give substance and shape to our glimpses of that love.

My own concern that theology can become presumptuous if it makes over-confident claims for itself and that we therefore need to develop a flexible approach to it such that it offers us a 'space for belief' is one that is shared – although their mode of expression may be a little different – by several distinguished figures of recent years. Indeed, the Maynooth-based Roman Catholic theologian, Martin Henry, has provided, in his significantly titled book *On not Understanding God*, what is almost a perfect complement to the idea outlined here of a 'space for belief'. In a discussion of the dogmatic tradition of the church he echoes Balthasar's phrase that dogmas are 'rather like fences around the mysteries', and he adds:

> They draw attention to where the mysteries lie but refuse ever to try to spell out their meaning definitively. In short, the church's dogmatic tradition is a tangible sign of how God is believed by Christian faith to lie beyond our comprehension.[2]

Within Henry's fences, and equally acknowledging the ultimate incomprehensibility of God, lies our space for belief.

A similar flexibility, this time rooted overtly in the fallibility of all human thinking, and especially our thinking of God, was argued for particularly cogently in an earlier generation by Alec Vidler in an appended note to Joseph Sanders' essay in *Soundings*. Of the authority of the church and of the theology which flows from that authority Vidler comments perceptively:

> At any given time the church, using the resources of scripture, tradition and reason, through the ministry of the hierarchy, of pastors, evangelists and theologians, and through the witness of the faithful, has adequate authority to bring home

to mankind the gospel of God and to build up those who respond to it in the Christian way of common life and obedience. But to claim *absolute* authority for itself or for any element or organ within its constitution is to make itself into an
idol and to usurp the prerogative of the Holy Spirit ... No definitions made by the church *in via* are in themselves final or
irreformable, however faithfully they serve to mediate to
mankind the final authority of God for practical purposes ...
Articulated credenda may always be susceptible of improved expression in the light of theological reflexion and
may require revision in the light of new discoveries.[3]
(Vidler's italics.)

What both Henry and Vidler are conveying in their different
ways is the simple reality that any theological position which
the church may espouse cannot ever be regarded as absolutely
definitive or final for the very good reason that (as we shall
argue more fully later) the doctrine of God is not the same thing
as God himself: it is, as Michael Adie so colourfully puts it,
merely an 'aide-memoire' to 'try to encapsulate and remind us
of a corporate and accumulated experience.'

In practice this means that because we can and must recognise the provisionality of all of our theological statements, we do
not have to be over-defensive or exclusive about any of them. If,
in theology, we are dealing with matters which are, in the last re-
sort, beyond our full comprehension, then we cannot claim an
absolute or objective 'rightness' for any one position. We may
wish, for the sake of order, and because we feel that certain insights are more inspiring or creative or internally coherent than
others, to indicate a preference for one set of ideas over another –
these ideas, once they are generally accepted, becoming what
may be regarded as orthodoxy – but this does not mean that we
have thereby absolutely to deny the validity of other positions.
There may well be genuine, even if partial, insights (and ones
which have been neglected in the 'mainstream' tradition) in formulations which lie outside the official expressions of the theological point in question.

The truth of this is readily demonstrated by a brief excursus into the patristic era. The early centuries of the history of the church are littered with attempts to do justice to the person and work of Jesus Christ, whether in himself or in his relationship to the Father within the Trinity, and to establish the relationship between human freedom and divine grace – to identify only two of the many issues which were so passionately at stake. So significant were these debates that the names of the the protagonists still resound in the ears of theology students today. Arius, Apollinarius, Athanasius, Pelagius, Augustine *et al*. Of these figures, a select few have passed the test of orthodoxy, while the remainder have been consigned to the 'sin-bin' of history as heretics, sometimes well-meaning ones perhaps, but heretics nonetheless, and therefore only ever to be refuted.

This is a situation which should rightly make us uneasy. All of these thinkers, and many more, were endeavouring to make some sense of the astonishing revelation of God in Christ and its consequences for the rest of humanity – a task which we have already seen is ultimately beyond our grasp. This fact alone should alert us to the realisation that no formulation is ever going to encapsulate perfectly in an objective once-and-for-all fashion the exact truth about Jesus Christ or any other aspect of the nature or activity of God. Even the best of patristic (or any other) thinking will only ever amount to an approximation towards what is glimpsed of the truth. This by itself might dispose us to feel a little more sympathy towards the losers in the history of doctrinal studies: we can only ever be speaking of degrees of inadequacy, not of absolute rightness and wrongness. Furthermore, from our perspective, even if one position might have seemed self-evidently 'right' fifteen hundred years ago in another culture and using different categories of thought, that is no guarantee that this same position is still adequate – let alone 'right' – today. Thus we may, for example, appreciate the insights of Greek metaphysics, but still feel that other thought categories (for example psychological ones) need to be invoked today to offer a picture of Jesus (or of human nature) which is compelling, (although of course still not absolute) in the present generation. This too might lead us to look with a more favourable eye on those whom history has so readily labelled as heretics: if the orthodoxy of fifteen hundred years ago needs restatement, then it might also be true that whatever their failings, some or all of the 'heretics' may offer – even perhaps amidst much that we feel to be unsatisfactory – some gems which are worthy of recutting and repolishing for present use.

It should be pointed out once again at this stage that this is by no means the same as suggesting that in matters theological 'anything goes'. It does matter that our theology reflects, as we have consistently argued in this study, what we perceive, through study pursued in prayer and under God, to be the best of our thinking, and clearly anything which is incoherent or which engenders unwholesome fruits is thereby to be discounted. Similarly, it is highly likely that there will always be certain insights which do appear to speak as adequately as it is possible for human thought and language to do so about God, and to disclose to us something of his nature, will or activity, and these moments of inspiration will always belong to the central core of Christian belief to which we may still wish to attach the shorthand soubriquet of 'orthodoxy'.

However, much of our theologising will lie between these two extremes, displaying moments both of illumination and deep darkness, and the imperfections of a theology, even if there are many of them, are no reason to write off the value of the whole, whether that be a theology from the patristic sin-bin or a more modern theology. An excellent contemporary example of this would be Don Cupitt, whose theology has been dismissed by the more conservative elements in the church, and who has been dubbed the 'atheist priest'. However, as I argued at length some years ago in *Don Cupitt and the Future of Christian Doctrine*, there is a real value in Cupitt's theology: not because I believe him to be correct at all points, far from it, but because his questioning and challenging of received positions is a necessary spur to a church which needs to rethink a good deal, however unwel-

come and painful that may be. However misguided I believe
some of Cupitt's answers to his questions may be, the fact remains that many of the questions he poses for the church are
entirely valid, and his work cannot simply be ignored or condemned as 'eccentric' or wrong, but has instead a real contribution to make to the contemporary and future theology of the
church.

Just as I am not arguing that 'anything goes', neither am I advocating the abandonment of a general consensus as to where
the most satisfactory and coherent explanations of different
theological issues lie, a consensus to which we may continue to
give the name 'orthodoxy'. I am merely arguing that the existence of an agreed orthodoxy should not automatically consign
every deviant opinion, no matter what its own internal merits,
to the theological Gehenna of heresy. We may well wish to continue to identify an agreed orthodoxy, but this does not mean to
say that we must deny all the insights of others, for even
Pelagius had, and still has something valid to say in the face of
the steamroller of Augustinianism. 'Heretics' may be, as someone once remarked, 'God's gift to the church'.

In the light of all of the foregoing, and if theology is going
successfully to perform such a function as we have outlined for
it here, I would plead for a tentativeness and a humility in all of
our theological thinking. Such an attitude is entirely appropriate
as we remember in all of our theological thinking that, as we remarked briefly above, God and our doctrines concerning God
and his will and activity are not the same thing. This ought to be
obvious, but one might be forgiven for thinking that, for most of
the church and for most of the time, the fact had been forgotten
entirely. Thus there appears to be precious little of such a spirit
of provisionality behind the pronouncements of the Roman
Catholic *magisterium*, or the arguments about almost every kind
of moral position within the Anglican communion, or the doctrinaire fundamentalism of many of the more extreme church communities. All, although it may manifest itself in very different
guises, are tarred with the same brush: all are certain that they

have drunk at the well-spring of absolute and divine truth, and all are apparently unaware of the fact (or have conveniently chosen to ignore it) that by the time its waters actually reach us they have been mingled already with the more brackish waters of the human mind and psyche. There is no such thing as absolute human knowledge of absolute truth.

Yet it is not only in our pronouncements that we tend to behave as though such absolute knowledge were available to us. We have an inclination to react to any supposed challenge or threat to those standards of absoluteness in exactly the same way. Any word spoken against the sacrosanct truths of our faith is felt as a direct attack on our security within that faith. Asking questions of our theological formulations, being provisional in our expression of them, or being willing even to contemplate any need for change in those formulations is seen as a sign of the erosion of faith or even as tantamount to blasphemy, as though being critical of our ideas about God is the same thing as giving God a dressing-down for his inadequacy in the role of the deity.

If we will look again, however, this is clearly not the case. Our theology can only ever be a human interpretation of our equally human glimpses of divinity, and as such it will always be inadequate. It will always stand in need of revision or modification in the wake of advances in our knowledge in other spheres or in the light of a creative illumination in our experience of God in prayer, worship or study.

Furthermore, neither does this provisionality and openness to change have to be perceived as threatening. It is only threatening if we conceive of our faith as being a handed-down 'deposit' – a spiritual package deal – which it is our duty to keep intact and to pass on in turn and in a similarly pristine condition to the next generation. In this case it is true that any talk of change will be seen as threatening to sully the purity or erode the fullness of that faith.

If, however, we can regard our own faith, and that of the whole church from its beginning until now, as a shared journey with and towards God, and a journey on which different people have glimpsed many things about God in varying times and places, then the picture changes somewhat. We are simply the inheritors of the shared fruits of that journey thus far, and we in our turn will be continuing that same journey with the possibility (and indeed the hope and expectation) of garnering further fruits along our way. Here, potentially, is a liberating openness to change. We are not attempting to safeguard what we have received, but to use it as a guide on our continuing journey (and exposing it to the hazards of that same journey) in the hope that what has been received by us will be in turn renewed by us and passed on, not as a fossilised 'deposit', but as a living faith in a God who is still to be found and experienced. And who knows, along the journey we might even find that we have made some small progress towards the better understanding of God, and discovered that it is by acknowledging the inadequacy of all of our thinking that we are set free from the prison of dogmatism and enabled to move with greater freedom in our space for belief.

It might, indeed, be no bad thing if the provisionality for which we have argued became not merely an ever-present, but also a much more prominent feature of our theological thinking, such that our whole theological framework might be underpinned (if that is the appropriate word!) by a standing acknowledgement that in any part of it – or even in the whole of it – we could be mistaken. To acknowledge this is not in any way to lessen our commitment to our faith, or our belief that, however inadequately, our theology does speak to us of real and important things. I may be willing to die for what I believe passionately to be the truth, but that does not ever rule out the possibility that I might be misguided. Utter commitment and thoroughgoing provisionality are not mutually exclusive. It is rather that if, even from the heart of my commitment I can still recognise that there is a gap between what I claim to be committed to and all of our human perceptions and formulations of that reality, then the way is at least opened to the possibility of development or change, in the absence of which possibility anything, theology included, is in imminent danger of petrifaction.

Finally, we have commented earlier on the relationship between any particular approach to theology and its fruits in practical Christian living, and it may be that it is in this context that
provisonality reveals its true value. Two of the areas in which a
rigid understanding of theology is most deleterious are the
minefield of ecumenical relationships and the effects of religion
upon the human psyche. In terms of ecumenism, provisionality
(as we will argue more fully in Chapter Seven) should engender
a little more humility when it comes to thinking of other
Christian traditions than our own – and indeed of the other
great religious traditions also; and the human psyche (to which
we turn next) is arguably better able to grow towards wholeness, and so towards God, in the freedom of a space for belief
rather than in the fortress (or prison, depending on one's perspective) of theological impassibility.

CHAPTER SIX

Theology and the Human Psyche

In Chapter Three of this study we have already cited Alister McGrath's contention that theology shapes what we do, insofar as it is the ultimate foundation for our attitudes, ideas and values as Christians. The point has come at which we need to move even beyond this and suggest that it also profoundly influences what we *are*. That this should be so is hardly surprising, for we can see the same process at work in many widely differing spheres. Our identity, and not merely our actions, is always affected and sometimes deeply moulded by the culture, expectations and general mores which surround us. We know this to be true within ourselves, and not infrequently it is so evident that others notice it as well. We may take one look at someone and say to ourselves: 'He must have been in the army!', or, as once happened to me when attending church on holiday dressed in very casual holiday clothes: 'Where are you the Rector of?' Likewise our personality is formed at least in part by the schools we attend, the organisations we belong to, the people we associate with and so on. It is only to be expected, therefore, that something as far-reaching, and which deals with such momentous matters as the church and its doctrines, should, if we once become a part of it, make a significant contribution to establishing who we are as well as merely what we do.

This contribution may be either immensely positive or crushingly negative depending on the extent to which different possibilities within the Christian tradition are emphasised or explained, and the extent to which we internalise these different aspects of the tradition. Michael Mayne characterises these two extremes aptly:

Much of my time is spent with individuals who have never really been able to love themselves, who feel unloved, unspecial and of little value. Some have never been on the receiving end of being loved for their own sake, even as a child. Many see God in threatening, judgemental terms. Many have damaged feelings and feed on guilt. There is only one truth I know that takes on such feelings at sufficient depth, that challenges them on their own terms and neutralises the poison. It is the truth that dawned on those who met and spent time with Jesus of Nazareth: who watched him as he encountered damaged people, sinful and perplexed people, and told them they were loved. Told them God even cared about the death of a sparrow. In the most perceptive of all the gospels, that of John, the message is plain: we may journey through the world as those who are valued and loved. Despite what we are. Despite all life's unpredictable and sometimes cruel nature. We are not to doubt that we are loved.[1]

This is a general assessment of the potential of Christianity to influence the psyche positively (when used properly) or negatively (when presented in a distorted manner). In a much more specific and extended discussion of one particular incidence (in this case negative) of such influence, Harry Williams, in his essay in *Soundings* entitled 'Theology and Self-Awareness', considers acerbically and yet also accurately, the potential effect upon the psyche of Cranmer's theology as expressed in the Eucharist in the *Book of Common Prayer*. His analysis is perceptive (and disturbing enough) to deserve quotation at some length:

The God, for instance, of the *Book of Common Prayer* seems sometimes to be a merciless egocentric tyrant, incapable of love, and thus having to be manipulated or cajoled into receiving his children. It is one thing to make a straightforward confession of sin as is done in the Confiteor at the beginning of the Roman Mass. It is another thing altogether to harp continuously and at length upon our utter unworthiness to approach God, as is done in Cranmer's Communion Service.

The general confession, with its repeated and elaborate protestations of guilt, looks like a desperate attempt to persuade God to accept us on the score of our eating the maximum dust possible. Even after the absolution we are uncertain whether we have succeeded in our project. We must be reassured by four quotations from scripture. The words of our Saviour Christ are not enough. They must be reinforced by what is said by St Paul and St John. This repeated affirmation of what is claimed as a certain fact indicates, and must often produce, doubt of its truth. One would not, for instance, in an airliner feel very comfortable if an announcement that all was well was made twice by the pilot, then by the wireless operator, then by the stewardess. One might be excused for fearing that something was seriously wrong. It is inevitable that what looks like Cranmer's deep lack of faith in God's mercy should communicate itself to many who use his liturgy, and should produce in them that spirit of bondage again unto fear from which Christ came to deliver us. This is all the more likely with the Prayer of Humble Access coming between the Sanctus and the Consecration Prayer. Unless, to the very last, we assure God of our unworthiness so much as to gather up the crumbs under his table, he may lock the dining-room door in our face.[2]

And the effect of all this upon the psychological state of the believer?

… who knows how many … have been caused to stumble by our incomparably unChristian litugy? If they were aware of the harm done them, it would matter less. But they are not. They cannot diagnose their servile attitude, their inability ever to presume anything good about themselves, as that which prevents them having life, and having it more abundantly.[3]

Williams takes his argument no further than this, although his conclusions are damning enough even so. For the purposes of his article it is sufficient for him to elucidate how our theological

assumptions influence us, with reference only to this one example of Cranmer's Holy Communion service. The full picture is
much broader than this though, and I propose to examine here
in some detail how the two very different approaches to theology,
delineated in the previous chapter, are likely to impinge upon
our perception of ourselves, upon who we feel ourselves to be,
and through this upon our psychological and spiritual 'wholeness'. Even at this level of detail the exercise involved here is still
only a partial one, for I am concerned only with the effects of a
whole scheme of church teaching and our approach to it, and
this does not account for the distinctive effects upon us of specific
aspects of theology such as Williams' article provides in probing
the links between guilt, fear, anger, confession and human
wholeness.

Leaving to one side, then, the influence upon us of specific
doctrinal formulations, we have identified in the previous chapter two contrasting attitudes towards theology, one provisional,
flexible and even tentative; the other inclined towards absoluteness, strictness and rigidity. How, then, might each of these be
characterised in terms of the impact it will tend to have on the
personality and well-being of its adherents?

Perhaps the first distinguishing feature of the effect of a more
rigid and dogmatic approach is that it is likely to engender a set
of very specific and precisely defined beliefs and attitudes.
There is little room for uncertainty and even less room for serious challenge or debate. The church, through revelation, and
most especially through the revelation of the scriptures seen as
directly divinely inspired, has direct access to the truth of things
and to the knowledge of God's will and commands, and there is,
from within this perspective, no means of gainsaying the position. It is, once accepted, an ethos which encourages a firm conviction that we know what is right and wrong, not merely on the
more obvious and commonly agreed issues such as murder, but
also on infinitely complex moral, social and psychological issues
such as the finer points of medical ethics or the legal framework
which ought to surround and safeguard expressions of human

sexuality. Similarly, it is an ethos which reassures its adherents that, as we saw in the previous chapter, they are 'in' and those who do not share their views and beliefs (all of them) are 'out' with all that that entails.

Furthermore, this hard and fast kind of framework both of belief and morality has a potential (all too often realised) to become, in itself and within the psyche of the individual, an excessively legalistic structure. Again this is hardly to be wondered at: after all, if we can even begin to suggest that we might know exactly who God is, then it is only to be expected that we might also know just what he wants of us. And so the 'laws' become ever more binding, with no room for manoeuvre or re-interpretation, and 'goodness' becomes, in a curious and ironic way, much more defined by negatives than by positives. Don Cupitt may be damning, but he is also on this occasion devastatingly accurate: '[Traditional Christian morality is] ... a matter of doing your best to avoid attracting God's displeasure, by reducing your sins to a minimum. It [is] ... a matter of working to rule, and keeping your head down and your nose clean.'[4]

In spite of Cupitt's strictures and the ironic inversion of what constitutes 'goodness', one might imagine that such an apparently secure and well-defined framework would provide a constructive and fruitful environment for the individual psyche, for by the same token we are often assured that children grow up to be more secure and happy in an environment which sets out the boundaries and which offers definite guidelines for behaviour. One might therefore expect that if this is a genuine characteristic of human nature, then adults would react in a similar fashion and grow to maturity of faith in a similarly structured environment.

What is omitted in this analysis, however, is the fact that that environment, whether for children or for adults, requires a degree of flexibility as well as restraint if it is to be genuinely creative. To continue the analogy with the upbringing and development of children, it is one thing to realise that a child has 'broken the rules' out of a sense of creative experimentation in a situation; it is quite another to condemn the child for 'breaking the rules' without even bothering to discern why the child might have done so or whether its motivation was culpable or not.

In all too many cases, it is, within the more strictly doctrinaire sections of the church, the second of these methods which is applied. The rules are there to be obeyed, and when they are broken the question of 'Why?' is not even on the agenda. All that is left is the appropriate (?) penalty for the misdemeanour committed.

Faced with a framework of this nature, there are essentially only two responses available to any individual: complete acceptance of what is very much a 'package', or outright rejection of it. Constructive criticism from within is not usually to be tolerated in the life of the more rigid varieties of faith community, as in their different ways dissident members of fundamentalist churches and several prominent Roman Catholic theologians have found to their cost. The concept of a 'loyal opposition' is not one which fits comfortably within this mind-set.

If then, it is to be accepted, the 'package' must be accepted unreservedly, and this brings with it certain almost inevitable consequences for the psychology of its adherents. Clearly there will be exceptions to any rule, and I am not claiming accurately to describe the mental and spiritual identity of every member of every variety of highly structured and doctrinaire religious community. I do suggest, however, that such communities do at least tend to inculcate certain views and patterns of thinking which will, to an extent which will vary with each individual, impinge on the entire self-understanding, outlook and psyche of that individual.

Thus a framework of clearly defined beliefs and rules which must not be broken lends itself first to the formation of a submissive frame of mind, or perhaps indeed it attracts those who are already instinctively submissive. Either way, such an attitude is assiduously fostered as a positive virtue. The 'faithful' are those who do not step out of line or ask awkward questions. Running alongside this positive rewarding of submission, as a kind of

darker parallel of it, is a sub-stratum of fear: the fear of the consequences of transgressing the rules. In past ages this fear was a
powerfully physical fear of bodily punishment: torture and
burning at the stake being among the favoured means of ensuring compliance among the faithful. Today the consequences are
more subtle but still very real, often involving some form of
public humiliation within the community and a demand for re-
cantation, and including as the ultimate weapon, the threat of
expulsion from the community, an expulsion which, of course,
removes one from the ranks of the blessed and places one
among the doomed – which, if one holds this sort of doctrine of
salvation and ecclesiology at all, amounts to a fairly potent reason for behaving oneself and submitting to the demands of one's
community.

A further danger of this carrot and stick of submission and
fear is that it will militate in favour of the creation of an unthink-
ing attitude towards one's beliefs and moral standards. Don
Cupitt has characterised this as a 'slave mentality', and while I
would not agree with his claim that Christianity is programmed
almost always to inculcate it in its believers, it is nonetheless an
accurate assessment of the effect of a particular interpretation of
Christianity. For church communities which subscribe to this interpretation, our business is simply to take orders and obey
them, the orders of course emanating ultimately from God himself, even if they are necessarily mediated through some sort of
church hierarchy.

This mentality is at once the vehicle of an implicit theological
statement – and, I firmly believe, a pernicious one – and a statement about our own self-esteem and capability. Thus God is
seen as the sole fount of everything. All the initiative is his. He is
the instigator of all things and we are simply the recipients of his
will and instructions. There is no sense in which we are seen as
'co-workers' with God, and no real allowance is made for
human creativity in partnership with God. We are incapable of
such creative partnership: our role, and the limit of our ability, is
obedience. Theologically this flies in the face of some of the pro-

foundest insights both of creation and Incarnation, and psychologically it says little for our estimation of our value and our sense of self-worth.

Although it is directed principally towards ensuring the compliance of the individual, this cocktail of submission and fear also has its impact on what might be called the 'corporate psyche' of the community. Like the individuals within it, the community as a whole will tend to become passive. It will be resistant to change and will tend to view change as being the equivalent of decay. There will be little or no questioning of received positions and traditions, and there will be no encouragement within the overall life of the community to think creatively or to take risks. The *status quo* is seen as being divinely ordained, and the aim is its ongoing maintenance.

This complex of submission and fear is only one aspect of the effect of a thoroughgoing dogmatic stance. A second feature of the outlook of this kind of faith community is its attitude towards those who are outside it. Again, generalisations are dangerous and there will always be exceptions, but an underlying characteristic of many such communities – not only in their more formal statements but also in the less formally expressed mores of their individual members – is an element of judgement-alism towards all who do not fully share their position. This judgementalism is both theological and ethical. Variations in belief are not merely differences of opinion or alternative ways of trying to express our response to the truth we have grasped: they are heresies. And likewise any touch of liberality – or even the gentlest questioning of received opinion – in ethical matters is contrary to the will of God which has already been divined with perfect clarity. Those who are 'out' are not simply non-members, they are beyond the pale, and this perception may well be manifested in a refusal – which I have witnessed on several occasions – to participate in ecumenical events. We will consider the theme of ecumenism more closely in the next chapter, but here it is sufficient simply to note this exclusivist and judge-mentalist tendency of rigid faith communities.

The third and final pyschological mark of this type of community which I propose to discuss here is something of a paradox. It might be thought that living in a clearly defined and closely bounded theological and moral world would, whatever its defects, at least impart the benefit of security. For the most part, however, the reality is precisely the opposite: both communities and the individuals within them tend to be insecure to a conspicuous degree. At first sight this may appear somewhat strange and surprising, but in fact it is precisely what one might expect, and it stems from what has come to be called in the context of Ulster Protestantism (itself often a good example of the kind of faith community I am describing) the 'siege mentality'. Thus, communities of this kind have cut themselves off from those outside and retreated into the holy fastness of their theological and moral fortress. They have been driven into the fortress by fear of contamination, but the real problem is that once you live in a fortress there is always the possibility that one may be trapped there or that someone may conquer it. Indeed, for most of this sort of community, there exists, I suspect, a strong feeling that 'the world' is holding the fortress in a state of permanent siege. The predicament is endless and self-propagating: one lives in a fortress because one is afraid, but by the mere fact of living there (in what can also so easily become a prison rather than a fortress) the fear is thereby reinforced.

At all points, then, any policy of theological and moral inflexibility would seem to run counter to several of our deepest requirements for spiritual health and wholeness. Certainty may sound an attractive goal, but it appears that it can only be purchased at the expense of inflicting some severe wounds upon the psyche of the individual and upon the corporate psyche and life of the church.

If this is so, and if, as we have argued earlier, such certainty is, properly speaking, unavailable to us anyway, given the limits of human knowledge, then what of the more provisional approach to theology which we have advocated in this study? What are some of its distinguishing characteristics, and what consequences is such provisionality likely to have for the psyche of the individual and for the church as a whole?

As it is a more open and flexible approach to belief and morals, so it has a less absolute attitude towards its own author-ity and towards the sources of that authority. As stressed in the previous chapter, this does not amount to an 'anything goes' scenario: it simply means that nothing – not even scripture – can be seen as providing a source of absolute and unambiguous di-vine commands on theological or moral issues. Whatever is said in scripture, even where we are dealing with such apparently 'direct' communication as God's inspiration of the prophets or the reported words of Jesus, has still been transmitted to us by the agency of human beings. It has passed through their con-sciousness and will inevitably have been shaped by this in the process of transmission. We do not have – and neither, as we have commented earlier, is there any possibility of our having – direct access to the 'truth' about God or about anything else. What we have are our human perceptions and glimpses of that truth which will always be partial and provisional, and given that this is the case, we have the privilege (and indeed the duty) constantly to test and to question these perceptions and glimpses in the hope that they may be thereby clarified even a little further – remembering always that this clarification is then itself equally provisional and open to continued debate and question.

A topical example of this process at work in the moral realm (and having bearing also on the theological) is homosexuality.[5] A more traditional approach based on the notion of an unbend-ing and unvariable divine command would condemn all homo-sexual activity as rejected in scripture and therefore by God him-self. If one is not entirely happy with this position, then in oppo-sition to it there are at least two possible lines of response. One is to argue as, for example, Michael Vasey[6] has done, that the scriptural evidence is by no means as clear cut and unambigu-ous as we have usually supposed, and that there are different ways of reading the supposed 'proof texts' which shed rather a different light on the subject from that to which we have become accustomed. An alternative approach – with which, I have to confess, I am myself more at ease – is to acknowledge that the biblical texts do intend to say what they appear to say, but to argue that what these texts therefore represent is one human interpretation of the will of God as glimpsed by particular individuals and cultures. In the face of this we are therefore entitled to examine the issues afresh and attempt to see whether we can find an alternative approach which is faithful to what we perceive of God and which reflects what we might infer would be the will of such a God. We might, in fact, want to apply an entirely different (although yet in fact equally scriptural) moral standard – and why should we not do so? A straightforward condemnation of homosexuality begins from the 'knowledge' of what God has 'said' – but as we have argued, both this 'knowledge' and this 'speech' are mediated through human agency. Why should we not begin not with what God is supposed to have 'said', but with the nature of God as we perceive him to be, and ask what possibilities this might open up for an alternative ethical approach to the subject?

If then, we are going to take as our starting point the 'nature' of God, prior to any specific claims about particular actions or speech, then a thoroughly scriptural place to start – and one which has resonated in the hearts of believers from the very beginning of our faith – is with the insight that if we can say anything at all about God, except that he is, then we must say that God is love. Admittedly in saying this we cannot be entirely certain what love in its fullness entails when applied to God, but we must assume that whatever the reality of this love turns out to be, it will be something more and not something less than we can imagine or than any value which we can put on it. If, in reflecting something of the nature of God, love is perceived to be the ultimate moral value then it is at least possible that the question of the moral status of homosexuality needs re-phrasing. It might be that we should be asking not is this right or wrong by some absolute *a priori* standard, but instead, what appears to be the most loving standard by which we ought to regulate our actions? Is it possible that a real and genuinely self-giving love between two people of the same sex might not after all be so wrong as we have so often assumed it to be? Might that relationship, precisely because of its love, be accounted something moral rather than something immoral? Lest this might seem to be merely a radical attempt to chafe a tender spot, it is worth repeating the words of John Barry writing as Cromlyn in the *Church of Ireland Gazette*, remembering that Barry is a retired 'seventy-something' rather than an awkward 'forty-something':

> ... one can have a life-long and monogamous commitment to self-giving and sharing between two people of the same sex (be they men or women) made in the sight of God and fulfilled within the life and worship of the church – occasionally in a manner far superior to some heterosexual marriages over which the church has been glad to preside.[7]

In posing these questions and outlining a different method of approaching the issue, I am not attempting to claim any particular 'rightness' for the above method, but merely indicating that the topic is a larger (and less closed) one than a more rigid theological and moral framework might suggest, and that there are benefits to be gained by allowing ourselves to continue to ask questions and allow for a measure of flexibility in our beliefs and ethics.

This relaxation and withdrawal from any claim to absolute authority which makes possible the more open approach which we have outlined here, has a further and liberating consequence for us. It is simply that if our theology (and with it our understanding of and approach to ethics) is only that – our theology – and not the absolute guaranteed truth about God and every aspect of his will, then in view of our human frailty, we may realistically expect to find ourselves to have been mistaken from time to time. We may even turn out to have been mistaken not merely on minor matters of interpretation but on issues of real substance which have had major and often tragic repercussions on the lives of men and women. We can assume, for example, that the wholesale importation of western European culture into much of Africa during the great missionary journeys of the mid-nineteenth century was performed with only the highest of motives, but the fact remains that for many African people the benefits of the gospel were outweighed by the destruction of much of their society and culture and the importation of new and fatal diseases. It is easy enough to look back and see where past generations have been in error, but in the main it is less easy to identify our own mistakes. All that is certain is that we shall have made them and will no doubt continue to go on making them, and this knowledge should in turn help to reinforce the provisionality of all of our theological and moral thinking – there is no aspect of it in which we are free from the possibility of error.

This potential for error is a curious case of what sounds initially like bad news turning out in fact to be good news. It is good news because we may reasonably assume that what we know about ourselves – that is, our propensity to well-intentioned error – God also knows. We may assume that God 'expects' these mistakes and that actions and understandings undertaken 'in good faith' are not culpable even if their consequences turn out to be undesirable. This would appear to square also with our apprehension of God as revealed in Jesus Christ: those who approached him 'in good faith' were never turned away, no matter what their sins or deficiencies, and his condemnation was reserved only for those who were too certain of their own rightness or righteousness. If this is the case, then we are freed to have a more relaxed attitude towards our own thinking, We are set free to be creative and open to experimentation as we seek to understand God and his will for us, expecting not God's condemnation of our wrongdoing, but his understanding and forgiveness of our inevitable errors as we grapple with so much that is at the limits of – and indeed not infrequently beyond – our comprehension.

This freedom is far-reaching in its implications, and it harmonises well with insights derived from a number of theological and scriptural sources. At the heart of this freedom is the fact that we are empowered to take the risk of thought. We are not merely to be the passive recipients of a body of knowledge or of faith or of anything else. We have been endowed with the capacity for questioning and creativity and we have not just the privilege but also the responsibility (even the obligation) of employing this capacity in the realm of faith as in every other aspect of our lives. We are encouraged to escape from what we have characterised as a 'slave-mentality' and allow ourselves to enter into a genuine partnership with God in the discerning and working out of his ongoing creative and loving will.

Such partnership and creative freedom is far from being 'heretical'. It is, on the contrary, thoroughly grounded both in scripture and in the framework of theology itself. There is no merit in an exhaustive analysis of every relevant scriptural text, and it is sufficient here briefly to cite one Old Testament and one New Testament passage in support of this position. It is thus firmly rooted in the Genesis accounts of creation and in the developed doctrine of creation. In both of the stories of the creation in Genesis chapters one and two the human race is given a divine command to exercise responsibility over the creation, and both the creation itself and the human race are, as it were, endorsed with the divine seal of approval: 'And God saw that it was good.' This is not so say that the human race is not capable of the most grievous of faults and failings, and one cannot ignore the fact that almost from the start the 'career' of humanity has been disfigured by these faults. Both chronologically and ontologically, however, these faults are secondary, and they should not be allowed to obscure two essential features of the landscape of creation. First and foremost then, the accounts of creation endow the human race with responsibilities *vis-à-vis* the rest of creation, and set us in a creative partnership with God, mythically portrayed in Genesis as God delegates to Adam the task of naming all of the creatures: God may be the original creator, but once the creation is in being the human race has a significant part to play in the further development and coming to fulfilment of that creation.

Certainly we are accountable to God for our stewardship, but we are also free to exercise our own creativity in response to (and in harmony with) God's own creative will.

Secondly, this human creativity is, in its reflection of the divine creativity, enfolded within the intrinsic 'goodness' of creation, and exploration, experimentation and risk-taking are not morally culpable but are simply part of the wonder and mystery of what it means to be a human being. Indeed one may argue that as these gifts are part of the 'package' of creation they are themselves 'good'. At the very least we are given the freedom to rejoice in the essential 'goodness' of all that is, ourselves included, and to assume that whatever mistakes our risks of creativity may lead us into will be understood and thereby forgiven by the God who has taken the greatest risks of all in creation and redemption. Mistakes there will be, but it will often be better (and certainly more 'educational' or engendering of development) to have done something and have got it wrong than to sit frozen into immobility for all time by the conviction of our utter depravity and sinfulness which render us powerless to act for fear of incurring God's wrath.

If the story of creation is sympathetic to such an interpretation as this then the ministry and teaching of Jesus call us into yet a deeper partnership with God and into the exercise of the fullness of our human potential in imitation of Jesus. Indeed Jesus brings with him a degree of parity in this partnership which represents a new development in our relationship with God and which offers us a further degree of confidence both in being who we are and in the exercise of creative risk-taking and re-evaluation of our deepest insights and values.

It is always dangerous to cite the words of Jesus as reported in the gospels as evidence of anything, since even the most conservative of biblical scholars is usually hesitant to vouch for the absolute reliability of any specific saying, and it is even more dangerous to rely on St John's gospel in particular as there is good reason to doubt the historicity of most of the reported words of Jesus in that gospel. However, I would argue on two grounds that the issue of the historicity of this or that saying is not of material significance in this context. First, because the saying upon which I propose to draw is in keeping with the whole tenor of Jesus' ministry which was to bring his disciples to the point at which they shared as partners in – and indeed eventually 'took over' – his own ministry; and secondly because whilst St John's gospel may not be verbally historically reliable it would nonetheless seem to be the case that the whole gospel is an attempt to dwell on and to tease out the significance of Jesus' life and ministry, and to this extent it represents at least a glimpse of what first century Christians saw as their calling in following Jesus.

The saying in question, then, is John 15:15: 'I no longer call you servants, because a servant does not know his master's business. Instead, I have called you friends, for everything that I learned from my Father I have made known to you.' As a call to partnership it is of a piece with other utterances from St John's gospel such as the statement that the disciples will do the same things – and indeed even greater things – than Jesus is doing, and it is in keeping also with the exploration of oneness between Father, Son, Holy Spirit and believer in chapter seventeen of this same gospel. Jesus' disciples – and by extension we ourselves – are called into the freedom of Jesus' own creative service of his, and our, heavenly Father.

Furthermore, this freedom is open and empowering as far as both thought and action are concerned, and it is expressed in the risk-taking and re-evaluation to which we have already alluded. Throughout his ministry Jesus indicated – in word and in deed – that the venture of faith is not about clinging to old certainties but about discovering new and dynamic ways to the heart of God and his purposes. Thus Jesus fearlessly re-interprets the old Jewish law, and perhaps even more radically he re-values and reinterprets the social and religious ethos and morality of his time: the publican is nearer to God than the Pharisee; the Gentile displays a profounder faith than the Jew; and the leper and the outcast become the bearers of the signs of the dawning of God's kingdom, as indeed happens very specifically in St John's gospel in the story of the man born blind in chapter nine.

All of this might be all very well, but it would be of limited significance if it began and ended with Jesus himself, so it is of central importance that the New Testament gives indications, both in the words of Jesus and in the experience of the apostles that this pattern is to continue with them through the empowering presence of the Holy Spirit within them and among them. Again in St John's gospel Jesus reassures his followers that after his departure at the ascension they will not be left alone but will receive the Holy Spirit who will lead or guide them into all truth (16:13), and in the Acts of the Apostles, Peter, for example, experiences a profound reversal of values and attitudes following his vision in Joppa and meeting with Cornelius in chapter ten, and all of the disciples are involved in a similar overturning of received opinion as they gradually come to terms with the transformation of Saul into Paul. Following this pattern then, each individual believer is called out of the insecurity and immaturity of familiar false certainties and into the dynamic freedom – and admittedly also the discomfort and sometimes the disorientation – of divine creativity, revaluation and newness of life.

Just as a tightly controlled and repressive approach to theology has consequences not only for the individual believer but also for the church, so too this is the case with the more open framework which we have advocated here. Some of these effects have been commented upon already, but there is a further one which deserves at least a brief notice as it concerns the fundamental outlook and mode of activity of the church. Mention has been made of the 'siege-mentality' of closed systems and the consequent paralysis within a fortress – and then later probably a prison – of one's own construction; and the effect of a radically open-ended theological standpoint is to allow both the individual believer and the church as a body to leave that fortress-prison and to live as vulnerably as Christ himself in the world: vulnerable both to that world and to the discovery of the ongoing provisionality of any and every theological and moral position.

Springing the bars of the prison in this way is no less than an invitation to the church to take the risk of living. The church and its members individually are empowered to begin thinking, questioning and experimenting and to discover from within themselves the multifaceted richness of creative living – with all of its pitfalls and possibilities for error and even disaster – rather than being condemned to endure a gray monotone existence because passive obedience is all that is perceived to be required by a tyrant God. The requirement of such a church is not slavishly to believe certain things – although of course belief remains a significant entity, though of the second order rather than of the first order – but rather to live and to love creatively, revaluing the world through the eyes of divine love, and seeking for others and for ourselves that wholeness which God desires for his creation, and the pattern for which he has shown us in his Son Jesus Christ.

Some may object to the openness of this approach, and there may be many who will feel threatened by it as a world of supposedly divinely ordained certainties appears to melt away, but for myself I can only say that I hope to be judged on the well-meaning of my own – possibly many – mistakes, rather than to be found guilty of not using to the full the creativity and restlessness which has been vouchsafed to me and to the rest of the human race – presumably to some purpose – by our Creator.

CHAPTER SEVEN

Theology and Ecumenism

The gifts, for such they are, of creativity and restlessness are perhaps nowhere more in evidence and nowhere more in direct opposition to any rigid and over-formalised *schema* of theological thinking than in the area of the relationships between the churches. It is in this realm too that the effects of theology, whether for good or for harm, are most visibly present and in which the crisis in theology which was discussed at some length in Chapter One of this study is most acute. Specifically, in the present climate, which has recently been described as being something of an 'ecumenical winter', the principal danger is that as far as a number of churches are concerned, a closed theological system will gain increasing control or come to exercise an ever-growing stranglehold over church polity and inter-church negotiations. The result of this is likely to be as unattractive as it is obvious: the driving of an ever-deepening wedge between increasingly defensive, and therefore also antagonistic, churches.

Even in simple practical terms this possibility is damaging enough, but there is also a major theological issue at stake here which concerns both the nature and standing of theology as a whole, and also more specifically the status of any confessional statement of belief. Naturally enough such statements occupy a privileged place in the life of each particular church – try telling the average Presbyterian that the Westminster Confession should be abandoned, or the average member of the Church of Ireland (northern especially) that the Thirty-Nine Articles should be scrapped, and the truth of this will quickly become evident! More than this though, they equally quickly come to be seen as constitutive of a primary identity – and this identity is principally that of the particular denomination rather than the wider identity of being a Christian, and so there is a curious (and invidious) inversion of roles: I am an Anglican or Presbyterian or Roman Catholic first and a Christian only second. Perhaps this is less obvious from an English standpoint than an Irish one, but certainly in Ireland this inversion is self-evident whenever one fills in any form which asks you to state your religion. On several occasions I have answered 'Christian' and been told: 'No, it doesn't mean that. Are you Church of Ireland, Presbyterian, Methodist or Roman Catholic?' – all of which are classed in the popular mind as being different 'religions'. Denominationalism has replaced Christianity as the primary category of identity.

That this should have happened betrays a theological myopia at the heart of each of the churches, for unless we believe ourselves to have been divinely guided into the fullness of absolute and infallible truth then all of these confessional statements – and with them our separate ecclesial identities – must be considered to be, along indeed with all theological statements, of the 'second order' as has been mentioned in a different context in the previous chapter. This would appear, however, not to be the case, and one can only assume that for all too many of the churches there is a supposedly divinely guided certainty about their position.

If this is so, then the theological issue is immense indeed, for it is none other, odd though it may sound, than idolatry. Any church which considers its own position as absolute or infallible – even such an august body as the Roman Catholic Church – is in danger of this, for as soon as we set up any formulation of our own as primary then it immediately supplants the greater mystery of God, and our ideas, even and perhaps especially if we think they represent God, become a form of idolatry. Again the Irish context may prove instructive. At the Church of Ireland General Synod of 1999 a substantial report on sectarianism was presented which included, in a section, of which I was the author, entitled 'The Theological Status of Sectarianism' the following:

> Without this acknowledgement [of ultimate inadequacy and provisionality], at however deep a level, a position or stance is reified, losing its provisionality in the process, and becomes a stance of rightness, indeed even of 'righteousness', which it is then one's duty to uphold in the face of those who have now, by definition, become 'wrong' … A goal or an organisation (and a need to belong) which may even be 'good' in themselves, have been perverted by being given a greater and more absolute weight and significance than something which is purely human can ever properly or morally bear .... [and this is] a form of idolatry.[1]

This process may be particularly stark in this particular context where its consequences are so obvious and so damaging, but the same process is at work at least implicitly whenever any church or individual absolutises their own position or allows it to sit in judgement on the standpoint and convictions of another Christian community.

This process of over-assurance and certainty leading inexorably towards idolatry leads us back to our previous hints and glimpses of the need for provisionality and indeed agnosis or unknowing both in our formulations of faith and theology and in our setting of boundaries. As we have previously noted, however, there are many Christians for whom all talk of provisionality and agnosis is not merely tantamount to heresy but is felt as evidence of a perverse desire to dismantle the faith to which they cling. No less a theologian than Maurice Wiles has addressed precisely this issue and these feelings of threat in an article revealingly entitled, 'Belief, Openness and Religious Commitment'. In the course of this article he makes in particular three cogent points which are germane to the present discussion.

First he states, as has been argued previously in this study, that provisionality and agnosticism are not at all the same thing as 'selling the pass' to outside influences and are no bar to commitment:

> … a lack of certainty and an openness to change in Christian

belief need not be just a matter of accommodation to popular pressure; such an attitude can be grounded in a firm conviction about the nature of religious truth. My claim will be that an attitude to theological and religious belief that incorporates a considerable measure of agnosticism is the only responsible attitude to questions of truth in religion, and also that such an attitude is fully compatible with serious religious commitment.[2]

Secondly, and stemming from this he maintains the paradoxical strength of such a position:

… insistence on a strong dose of agnosticism as an essential component in Christian belief and commitment is admittedly not common currency in the life of the churches. But that is a sign of their weakness, not of their strength.[3]

Thirdly, and very importantly in the current climate of dialogue between the world faiths in which the 'truth' of religions other than one's own is a major factor, he argues for provisionality as perhaps the only means of maintaining simultaneously both the value of one's own religion and that of another:

... there are many who see themselves as orthodox Christian believers, but who yet conscientiously affirm the presence of truth in other religions. In view of the enormous differences of conceptuality and of beliefs between the major religions, there is, it seems to me, only one way such a position can be consistently maintained. If it is not to involve abandoning any form of realistic truth claim for religious beliefs altogether, we have to acknowledge that the truth of those affirmations which constitute the body of Christian beliefs must be of a highly partial and provisional nature. Any claim to certainty about the truth of one's own religious beliefs is flatly incompatible with the acceptance of more than one religion as in any serious sense a vehicle of truth.[4]

The full implications of this as far as the other world religions are concerned are outside the scope of this chapter, but it is important to note Wiles' point both for its own sake as identifying a positive meeting point for Christianity and the other world faiths (and indicating where a comparative theology might begin), and also because, in the context we have described, in which denominationalism comes to stand for religion, Wiles' remarks apply with their full force to the current ecumenical situation. Indeed it is hard to see how further substantial ecumenical progress might be made (other than of the 'lowest common denominator' variety, to which we shall return later) unless the various churches and traditions learn to embrace rather than to fear the notions of provisionality and agnosis and have the courage to allow theological matters to assume a second rather than a first order status.

If this change of status is made it is in no way to suggest that theology is no longer important. Rather, it represents a refusal to allow theology to play the role of tyrant over other areas of Christian life, and indicates a desire to allow other factors to weigh more substantially in the scales – an issue to which we shall return more fully in the final chapter. For this to happen, then, the churches need to place less stress on the necessity (and the assurance) of their theological and specific confessional statements being in some absolute objective sense right, and more emphasis on the value of Christian experience and especially of Christian love. It is the same equation in a somewhat different context as that which was discussed in Chapter One with reference to figures such as St Francis of Assissi and Marjory Kempe. It is not that experience must rule theology any more than theology must rule experience, but rather that the two must be held in creative tension such that each is allowed to inform the other; for just as unfettered experience is but a short step away from religious and spiritual chaos, so too an unchallenged and unchallengeable theology is likely to prove a sterile spiritual *cul-de-sac* as far as a living Christian experience of God and his purposes is concerned.

At the present moment the various churches (and perhaps because of its particularly power-oriented hierarchical structure the Roman Catholic Church most especially) would appear to be in something of a quandary on this issue, and the future viability – or at least credibility in the eyes of the majority of the faithful – of their theological structures may very well depend, as again was hinted in a more general fashion in Chapter One, on their response to it: that is, whether theology comes to inform and be informed by experience, or whether it seeks rigidly to dominate the whole life of the church and thereby inadvertently and ironically signs the death warrant of its own relevance.

Thus there would appear at this point in time to be two camps, each representing one pole of the theology / experience continuum, and the challenge for the churches is to develop sufficient flexibility of structure and theology (without abandoning these things altogether) to allow for a constructive meeting and dialogue between them.

At one end of the spectrum there is a number of church hierarchies, theologians and governing bodies – pre-eminent among them, but by no means alone, the Roman Catholic Church – which are adhering firmly to traditional confessional statements and standpoints and making these the authority by which experience is unilaterally to be judged. The Roman Catholic Church has been singled out because of the consistency with which this relationship between theology and experience has been articulated, although as we shall see it is not alone in tending towards this position.

For the Roman Catholic Church then, at least as far as the hierarchy is concerned, there has been no move, and as far as one can tell there will never be under the present regime (so recently renewed) any move, on two essential theological sticking points: the validity of the vast majority of ecclesiastical orders including Anglican orders, and the requirement that intercommunion must follow rather than precede theological agreement – it is a consequence of, rather than a contributory factor towards church unity. Thus, for example, there has never been any move, in spite of a number of so-called fraternal meetings between successive Popes and Archbishops of Canterbury, to rescind the

nineteenth century declaration of the invalidity of Anglican orders. (Incidentally, one might legitimately ask why, unless there
is some intensely convoluted double-think going on, various
Popes have been apparently so willing to meet with and even
lead worship with someone who is, technically at least, in their
eyes merely a prominent – and schismatic – lay person!) Similarly,
the traditional position on inter-communion has been very recently largely reinforced by the publication of *One Bread, One
Body* which has proved so disappointing and hurtful to many
Anglicans. It should be noted, of course, that it has proved
equally hurtful to many Roman Catholics, in particular those
who cherish the presence of their Anglican neighbours and
would wish to express those bonds of affection more fully, and
perhaps most especially of all by those who are married to
Christians of another tradition and who, if they are to obey the
discipline of their church, may share their lives, their feelings
and their bodies with each other, but may not share the fullness
of their common faith.

But the Roman Catholic Church is not alone in this quest for
the purity of theological isolationism. The structures are very
different, but in recent years and for different reasons, the
Orthodox Churches and the Presbyterian Church have dis-
tanced themselves from ecumenical bodies and associated ventures: the Orthodox Churches expressing unease with their position in relation to the World Council of Churches, and the
Presbyterian Church in Ireland taking the decision at its 1999
General Convention in Belfast not to associate itself with new ecumenical bodies in Great Britain and Ireland. Undoubtedly in
each case the issues at stake are complex ones, but behind all of
this complexity there stands the stark fact that confessional
boundaries have once again proved too strong to be overcome in
the service of the greater good of a profounder unity based on
Christian love rather than merely on the chimerical absolutes of
confessional dogmas.

At a structural and theological level, then, however this is expressed in any particular church, the various traditions continue

to be suspicious – or at least wary – of one another. At a very different level, though, the story is quite the opposite. For 'on the ground' congregations of all denominations are learning to live and work together ever more closely, sharing in common projects centred around social needs or outreach, joining together in community ventures, uniting for bible studies, Lent groups or informal worship groups, and expressing the fullness of this relationship in, although perhaps as yet infrequent, shared worship and intercommunion. Similarly inter-church families are regularly ignoring the discipline of the Roman Catholic Church especially, and worshipping together and receiving Holy Communion together in Anglican, Presbyterian and Methodist churches. For all of these congregations, and there are many of them, experience, and especially the moving experience of meeting with God in one another and in shared worship, and thereby growing also in love, has been placed first, and just as love is said to cover a multitude of sins, so too it would appear, when it is allowed to do so, it has the power to cover a wide variety of theological differences.

By their actions, then, these congregations and individuals are making a powerful — and to hierarchies and governing bodies often an irritating and sometimes a threatening! – statement of intent that confessional and theological ties must be looser and less specific in order to facilitate the degree of unity which they themselves see as essential if Christianity is to be faithfully lived in mutual love 'on the ground'. One suspects that if such flexibility is not forthcoming, then with every further attempt to tighten the rules churches will discover that they have inadvertently shot themselves in the foot as opposition to such measures becomes more outspoken and rules are increasingly perceived as irrelevant and thereby ignored. The subject matter may be somewhat different, but the process is exactly that described so deftly by Stephen Sykes in connection with the doctrine of the Trinity: 'To many the doctrine of the Trinity has seemed too erudite to be relevant; and in truth theologians have not always avoided a self-defeating level of detailed pseudo-precision.'[5] Precisely. The more detailed and restrictive confessional statements and rules become, the more 'pseudo' they are likely to seem to those to whom they were intended to apply.

Like these many faithful Christians who are simply 'getting on' locally with the business of ecumenism, then, I am not looking for or seriously expecting – in the short term at least – any full measure of theological agreement between the churches, although steps have been taken and continue to be taken in this direction. More particularly, I would not wish to advocate any search for a theological lowest common denominator between the churches, as this is likely to result in a travesty of meaningful theology of a kind which allows us seriously to explore difference and draw together from the richness of our various traditions. The alternative, and altogether more creative picture would be something like that sketched out by Richard Jones in the excellent modern hymn *Come, all who look to Christ today*, verses three and four of which read:

> Come, young and old from every church,
> bring all your treasuries of prayer,
> join the dynamic Spirit's search
> to press beyond the truths we share.

> Bring your tradition's richest store,
> your hymns and rites and cherished creeds;
> explore our visions, pray for more,
> since God delights to meet fresh needs.

Thus rather than a colourless uniformity, I am arguing simply for an acceptance of, and indeed celebration of difference within the 'space for belief' of which mention has previously been made: an acceptance based on the recognition of two things: first, that of the provisionality of any or all of even our most cherished religious affirmations (especially when they are denominationally specific ones), and secondly, that of the need to allow the Christian experience of God present within the community to inform our theologising at least as much as our theology attempts to regulate and codify that experience.

Such a plea as this is, I would argue, at once more realistic
and in a curious way actually more honest than any demand for
full theological agreement before unity can take place. For there
are a number of problems inherent in any such demand, several
of which place a cumulative question-mark over the intellectual
and spiritual honesty of the demand, and one in particular of
which seriously challenges whether theological agreement before unity is ever likely to be a practical possibility.

The first two problems relate to the familiar notion that we
must all 'share a common understanding' before we can 'share a
common table', and both have ramifications which raise questions in connection with the issue of the visible or invisible nature
of the 'true church'. First, then, and trivial though it may sound,
it is a genuine ecclesiological issue, how does this proviso demanding a common understanding relate to individuals within
each communion who do not (or perhaps even cannot for whatever reason) share the fullness of that communion's doctrinal
understanding of the Eucharist? How many Roman Catholics,
for example, actually do 'share a common understanding' of the
Mass with the Pope or with the best Roman Catholic theologians
– and do the theologians share a common understanding with
the Pope indeed? If not, should they be debarred?

Secondly, and in a sense conversely, what about those who
overtly belong to a different communion but who may indeed in
all essentials 'share a common understanding' even though for
reasons of tradition or upbringing they may have remained in
that different communion? Simply because someone belongs to
a different communion – especially in the case of one so diverse
as the Anglican communion – how is it possible to know that
they do not share a common understanding with another tradition? Thus it may be, for example, that some Anglo-Catholics
might share a common understanding with many, if not perhaps all, Roman Catholics. As Cyprian and others discovered in
their generation, the invisible church can wreak havoc with the
apparently neat demarcations of the visible church.

The third problem, whilst of a different nature, also brings into question the appropriateness of demanding full agreement – or even anything like it – before a further degree of unity or intercommunion is officially sanctioned. This is the issue of precisely what is meant by 'full agreement': agreement with what and on whose terms? Again it perhaps seems unfair to single out the Roman Catholic Church for special notice, but the intention is in no sense to stigmatise that church. It is simply that the Roman Catholic Church has time and again had the courage of its convictions to lay down what it sees as the essential markers for unity, and it is self-evidently easier to comment on a church which has been overt in this way (just as it was in a previous chapter to comment on the relatively fixed forms of intercession within Anglicanism) than it is to discuss other churches which, whilst they may have an equally strong ethos have, in public at least, kept their heads down behind the barricades and said little or nothing about what their own preconditions for unity might be.

In the case of the Roman Catholic Church, then, in spite of all the progress made through the various Anglican-Roman Catholic International Commission talks and discussions with other ecclesial bodies, it most often appears that full agreement means full agreement with the present position of the Roman Catholic Church. It is hard to discern any significant moves by which Rome might come to agreement with the position of any other communion on matters of doctrine or order, or even come to some new position which might represent a common ground between Rome and another communion. 'Full agreement' all too often comes to mean – to all intents and purposes – full acceptance of the Roman Catholic position, and this is hardly an inspiring starting-point for any discussion of church unity or intercommunion.

Taken cumulatively, then, these three problems seriously vitiate the probity of any demand for full agreement. They suggest that it rests on a position which is fundamentally suspect on two counts: that of the practical impossibility of deciding, except in terms of the notoriously misleading 'visible' church who actually agrees with whom; and that of who dictates the terms of full agreement and what this sonorous phrase actually means when it comes to being 'cashed out' in ecumenical discussion.

Whether full agreement as a condition for unity and inter-communion is an intellectually honest or sufficiently Christ-like demand is, of course, a substantial enough question by itself, but alongside it there runs an equally compelling practical issue: that of what approach or strategy is, in the end, most likely to bear the desired fruits both of unity/intercommunion and a greater measure of theological agreement. In a sense the question is: which is most likely to be achieved for the sake of the other? Is agreement to be reached in order to produce unity, or is a greater measure of unity more likely to produce closer agreement?

It is hard to answer this question for anyone else, and it may be that in what follows I am speaking entirely for myself – although over twenty years of parochial experience and a wide variety of ecumenical contacts at a local level would tend overwhelmingly to confirm the fact that my own feelings would be shared by many others at the parochial coal face, both lay and clerical alike. Indeed the same issue, that of the purpose both of the church and of ecumenical endeavour, was raised by the Lambeth Conference of 1988 which commented succinctly:

> Too often the preoccupation with negotiations to restore the institutional union of denominations, separated in the distant past, has failed to capture the imagination and fire the enthusiasm of Anglicans. We need to ask what the church is for; and only if its purpose demands closer unity will we be moved actively to work for such unity.[6]

From a personal standpoint, then, it is one thing to study the theological stances and the confessional and sacramental statements of another tradition, and it is quite a different thing to experience them 'in action'. As a theologian – even a part-time one – I am, naturally enough, fascinated to discover more about other traditions than my own and other people's very different attempts to formulate their faith, but however well I may come to understand these they are no more than the outward shell of a particular tradition and expression of faith, and they are unlikely to 'move' me either emotionally or theologically – or at least not enough to modify my own views which have behind them all the feelings and religious experience of forty-five years as a worshipping Anglican. I may appreciate certain insights, but the experience of God is still likely to be located for me firmly within the tradition that I not only understand intellectually but have come deeply to love as having been the vehicle for my own relationship with, and experience of God to date.

Further than this, it would be difficult – though not, I have to admit, entirely impossible – for me to take the risk of possibly abandoning certain ideas or practices which have been valuable or have mediated the presence of God, in order to take the risk of a unity of whose ability to mediate that same presence I have as yet no knowledge. And by the same token, it would be equally difficult – though again, I suppose, not intrinsically impossible – to come to accept different interpretations from those with which I am so familiar without again any proof of their capacity to sustain me in a life-giving encounter with God. Perhaps I am a particularly dyed-in-the-wool Anglican, but agreement as a pre-condition for unity and intercommunion looks to me distinctly unattractive: at best a remote possibility, and at worst an ecumenically destructive piece of wishful thinking.

Conversely, my experience of working with people of other traditions, of sharing in their worship and sometimes in their sacraments, leads me to believe that, valuing this degree of unity as I do (along with many others), deeper theological agreement then becomes more and not less likely. For in experiencing the worship and sacraments of others I discover that their understandings, statements and interpretations are not merely arid and alien formulations, but that the worship and practices which are based on them in fact do result in a meeting with, and response to God in and through his Son Jesus Christ in the power of the Holy Spirit – perhaps even more powerfully than within the exclusiveness of my own tradition, for I am brought into sacramental contact with 'ecclesial strangers' and discover with renewed force the life enhancing and renewing power of the second of the two great commandments as well as the first, and strangers become neighbours in and through the act of sacramental sharing. This has, in fact, been precisely my own experience in my home parish at an event known as the 'Folk Mass', organized by the Roman Catholic parish, at which I and other parishioners have been positively encouraged to receive Holy Communion. Under these circumstances, knowing God in Christ to be at the heart of this worship – and therefore of the life of another church as much as my own – I am more likely to make accommodations and even sacrifices for the sake of the maintenance and furthering of this unity which I have come to experience and so to desire ever more deeply. On purely practical grounds then – although not unrelated to more spiritual matters there are good reasons for at least questioning whether full agreement before unity or intercommunion will ever prove to be an adequate vehicle for what may well prove to be increasingly delicately poised ecumenical negotiations in the future.

From an ecumenical viewpoint, as from the various other perspectives from which we have considered it, theology – or more correctly an over-insistence on the primacy of an unyielding theological system – gives rise to a number of intractable difficulties, and appears to be creating a morally and spiritually infelicitous climate for further discussion. If there is ever to be any further substantial progress towards unity – however one wishes to define that unity, either as some sort of organic institutional unity, or simply as an increased *koinonia* expressing itself in mutual recognition of sacraments and minstries between the various communions – then it would seem that there will have to be a new, and as in all creativity, risky, degree of flexibility somewhere. Further inflexibility will lead inexorably to a stalemate, from which escape will become progressively more difficult, and once again the fortress (this time of our denomination) will have become our prison.

What is needed, apart from courage and a willingness to take risks in the service of unity – the ultimate risk being, of course, that one's own cherished denomination may one day no longer be necessary and therefore cease to exist as a distinctive entity,

although one would hope that the best of its insights and spirituality would be retained in whatever form of church might succeed it – is once again what we have called here a 'space for belief'. Denominations, as well as Christianity *in toto* need constantly
(and consistently) to acknowledge that our human searchings
after divinity are all, by definition, inadequate. Similarly, if our
attempts to formulate what we know and experience of God are
inadequate, so too must be our church structures, confessional
identities and practices. At best they are only pale and partial reflections of the reality which they seek to illuminate and communicate.

Were this *proviso* to assume a greater prominence in the lives
of the churches, both at 'grass roots' level and especially among
hierarchies and governing bodies, then we might find that we
were able to discover in each other's traditions elements that are
– dare one say it! – more adequate than they are in our own. We
might even find ourselves able to meet around a common table
united in an awareness of inadequacy and in a new depth of
humility towards one another stemming from that knowledge
of inadequacy. And so in turn we might again recognise that
whilst our theology shapes our faith and guides our pilgrimage
yet it must never become so rigid that it blinds us not only to its
own provisionality, but even more importantly to the presence
of a God who is beyond all of our formulations and sometimes –
perhaps even pre-eminently – deigns to meet us most profoundly
at precisely those points at which all of our most finely-honed
words and concepts ultimately fail us.

The Place of Theology in Faith

It has been the consistent argument of this study that there needs, both for the sake of theology itself and for that of the church, to be a new balance found between theology and a variety of elements of church life, some of which have been touched on here and others of which have almost undoubtedly been overlooked. Perhaps it has seemed at times to some, and especially to those of a more cautious and conservative cast of mind, that the intention has been, by some sort of invidious process of attrition, to declare theology to be redundant. As this study draws to a close, perhaps now is the time to state clearly: not so at all. The criticisms which have been levelled at the practice of theology in the church have been, as they say, 'for its own good'. For it is precisely the argument of this study that, as was discussed in some detail in the Introduction and in Chapter One, theology is in severe danger of contributing to its own redundancy – or at least irrelevance – if it does not put its own house in order, and furthermore, that this irrelevance or redundancy would have profoundly deleterious effects on the life of the church. To expose theology to criticism – even severe criticism – is not the same thing as planning its demise: quite the opposite, in fact.

Thus, whilst critical of much of present practice, I am attempting – with no anti-theological hidden agenda – to argue for a revision of the current status of theology, and for a new and healthier balance between it and the Christian experience of God in all its forms. If this balance is to be achieved it is necessary to loosen the stranglehold which theology all too easily gains over church life: after all, the clearer the boundaries and the defini-

tions are, the easier it becomes for those who exercise organis-
ational control over the church, and as we have previously ob-
served, theology is always in danger of becoming a convenient
tool for the wielding of power and control.

The need, therefore, is for a more flexible theological approach which is more readily capable of assimilating and responding to what God might actually be doing now among his
people, and perhaps especially as we have seen, in the realm of
ecumenism; and if theology is to occupy such a position then it
cannot claim absoluteness for itself or stand as a kind of door-
keeper to Christian experience such that that experience can
only gain admittance to the household of faith if it can find the
right theological (or even confessional) password. Certainly
theology can and does assist profoundly in the interpretation of
that experience, but it cannot in an *a priori* fashion, simply dictate what experience of God may involve or how it must be
expressed.

So where does this balance lie? In essence it relies on two
complementary propositions, both of which are succinctly expressed, although in different discussions, by Alister McGrath.
First, the acknowledgement that theology remains vital to
Christianity as a framework to assist us in interpreting our experiences and glimpses of God, although, as we have consistently
argued, this framework must be flexible rather than unyielding:

> ... [Christian doctrine] is responsible and obedient reflection
> on the part of the church on the mysteries of faith. Doctrine
> preserves the Christian faith from woolly and confused un-
> derstandings of its identity and calling, and provides believ-
> ers with a framework for interpreting the ambiguities of
> human experience. It is the natural outcome of Christian re-
> flection on the mysteries of faith. It allows the ambiguities of
> human experience in the world to be interpreted and trans-
> formed. It opens the way to the construction of a worldview,
> through which Christian attitudes and approaches to a range
> of matters – spiritual, ethical and political – can be devel-
> oped.[1]

Secondly, and bearing in mind that key phrase, 'the mysteries of faith', there runs alongside this the paramount truth that God in Christ is the heart of our faith, and that that faith is expressed first and foremost in relational and experiential terms, and that furthermore the Christ whom we meet is prior to, and ultimately beyond all of our formulations about him:

> It is not so much 'articles of faith' which Christians have in common, but the redeeming presence of the risen Jesus Christ ... theologising is secondary to the Christian experience of Christ and appreciation of his benefits ... the primary *fundamentum* of faith is Jesus Christ, who is and will always remain prior to attempts to explain him.[2]

The setting alongside each other of these two propositions would, if it were to be done consistently at every level of the church's thought and practice, have significant and life-enhancing consequences both for the church's appreciation of its theology and its authority to teach and promulgate its doctrines, and also – in all likelihood – for the response of individuals both within the church and outside it to that teaching. From the church's own standpoint, the pressing need is for the church to learn to see its theology – and with it the authority by means of which that theology is taught and expounded – as being, whilst necessary, nonetheless provisional: as being what Alec Vidler called nearly forty years ago, although his words remain as fresh and as relevant now as then, adequate but not absolute. Thus as was discussed in Chapter Five, Vidler wrote in *Soundings*:

> At any given time the church, using the resources of scripture, tradition and reason, through the ministry of the hierarchy, of pastors, evangelists and theologians, and through the witness of the faithful, has *adequate* authority to bring home to mankind the gospel of God and to build up those who respond to it in the Christian way of common life and obedience. But to claim *absolute* authority for itself or for any element or organ within its Constitution is to make itself into an idol and to usurp the prerogative of the Holy Spirit. By refusing

to claim absolute authority for itself, the church witnesses to the continuing activity of the Holy Spirit who is ever guiding it into a fuller understanding of that truth which will be known completely or absolutely only 'at the last day'. No definitions made by the church *in via* are in themselves final or irreformable, however faithfully they serve to mediate the final authority of God for practical purposes ... Articulated credenda may always be susceptible of improved expression in the light of theological reflection and may require revision in the light of new discoveries.[3] (Vidler's italics)

Similarly, and arising out of this, a church which knows this to be true of itself and of its theology is likely to present a very different, and more attractive, face to the world than a church which lives within its own theological fastness. Marcus Braybrooke captures well a common reaction to a perception of the church (and with it the Christian faith) as consisting primarily in a framework of inflexible theological positions. He comments that too many people, '... have perceived Christianity as a list either of teachings to be believed or of enjoyable ways of behaving to be avoided'.[4] In contrast to this negative influence, it is to be hoped that if the centrality and priority of Christ and a relational and experiential faith such as McGrath speaks of were to be vibrantly re-discovered throughout the church, and the church was in turn to discern how to mediate that faith in renewed humility *viv-à-vis* its own limitations as Vidler wished, then people might be freed from their negative impressions of church and faith and given once again the vision that, '... revelation is not truth about God but encounter with the Living God',[5] and that similarly in its entirety, 'Christian faith ... is not, in the first instance, acceptance of certain intellectual dogmas, but trust in the Living God.'[6] Identifying the appropriate place for and character of theology in the life of the church is thus potentially far more than merely an academic exercise. It is, as we have argued from the outset of this study, vital to the effectiveness of the continued ministry and mission of the church.

To believe this and to say it is one thing; but to communicate

it vividly enough to bring the ideas behind it to life is quite another. For the sake of imbuing these particular dry bones with
life, two analogies to be contrasted with the present situation
might help to shed light on the kind of place and status being
advocated for theology. At present then, theology as we have argued, all too often seems to provide an unchanging and almost
juridical framework which dissects and codifies every aspect of
faith and which resists firmly – and usually successfully – every
attempt to change or modify that framework.

One alternative vision of the place and function of theology
might be to suggest that it should be somewhat in the nature of
an Admiralty Chart, which is as accurate as it can reasonably be,
and yet which is always provisional and in danger of becoming
outdated and therefore not merely useless but positively dangerous by, for example, the appearance of a new and currently
uncharted wreck, or the shifting of sand to open a new or close
an existing channel – and in connection with this analogy one
might add that we have seen in our discussion of the church's
public worship at least some of the problems that arise when an
outdated chart is in use.

A second possibility, if it does not smack too much of an un-
becoming levity, is that theology is in some respects not unlike a
weather-forecast. Again, it is as accurate as it can possibly be,
but it is only ever provisional, and therefore subject to constant
revision due to unpredictable factors: just as theology is necessarily provisional as a result of the constant presence of the 'God
of Surprises' at the heart of the faith which it seeks to delineate.

Finally, these analogies, with their insistence on the need for
constant updating, point to what is perhaps the ultimate reason
for seeking a reappraisal of the place and function of theology:
namely, that theology is always, by definition as a reflective activity, based on what God has done, and the primary reason
why it needs always to be flexible and to provide a 'space for belief' rather than a fortress-cum-prison, is that if it is to be true
both to itself and to the God who is at its heart, it is essential that
it should be ever open to what God is doing in the present and to

what he may do in the future. This dynamic connection of past, present and future is illustrated with particular incisiveness by Tom F. Driver in a discussion of the Christian response to Jesus. The passage is a substantial one, but it is deserving of full quotation:

> Insofar as our relation to the past is moral, it is reflective. Human life loses its moral quality when it is content with a reflexive use of the past. In everyday terms, this means repeating or perpetuating a course of action simply because it existed in the past. To be tradition-bound is to want to reflect (mirror) the past without critical reflection. Sometimes this posture results from sheer failure of imagination. More often it is a strategy for maintaining the power of an elite. Occasionally it is a necessary mechanism of survival, just as one's biological reflexes are designed to protect the organism by doing automatically what worked before. Indeed, there is a genuine motive of survival in all honouring of tradition. When a society or an institution, however, makes survival its main purpose and therefore tradition its main value, it begins to become immoral. When a church does so, it pulls away from resurrection faith, turning instead to a reflexive use of the past and an idolatry of memory. This is so even if the memory is of Jesus Christ.
>
> The main purpose of the church is not to remember Jesus. Its main purpose, surely, is to participate now, in present-future time, in the redemption of the world. To this end have the life, death, and resurrection of Jesus in past time been given. It is for christology and the churches to make a reflective, not a reflexive use of that gift. If we move in the freedom whereby the risen Christ is making us free, our continuity with Christ past will take care of itself. It is in any case not a continuity of letter but of spirit, and the right form of it will be revealed in the education of conscience by the sufferings of the present age. Such at least is the confidence I have that Christ is not dead and is therefore free to approach us in a form we cannot foretell.[7]

There is the heart of a living faith: that 'Christ is free to approach us'. That approach, made definitively in the Incarnation and made again and again day by day in the worship and daily experience of believers, is the primary *datum* of our faith, and theology exists, in all of its inadequacy and provisionality, not for its own sake but rather to facilitate and enable us to interpret that approach and subsequent encounter. The abiding pitfall, given the church's need for shape, organisation and coherence, is that theology can all too easily – and unobtrusively – become an apparently first-order activity, whilst in fact it needs to understand itself, afresh perhaps in each generation, as being a second-order activity. It stands behind, not in front of, whatever God is doing now, and behind also, therefore, the rich and life-enhancing experiences of God in the church. Theology must humbly wait upon God, rather than rashly attempt to encompass him, and in recognising this we must rest content with a degree – perhaps sometimes a large degree – of provisionality and a systematiser's nightmare of loose ends, lest, imprisoned in a specious tidyness of our own devising, we miss in our midst the glorious untidyness of God himself.

Bibliography

The following bibliography is not, in any sense, intended to be exhaustive. It is simply a list of a number of books which deal most interestingly with aspects of the Christian faith and their relations to theology such as we have discussed in this study. It is intended to be, not so much a scholarly reference tool, as simply a guide to further rewarding and enjoyable reading.

Michael Adie, *Held Together*, (London: Darton, Longman and Todd, 1997).

Paul Badham, *The Contemporary Challenge of Modernist Theology*, (Cardiff: University of Wales Press, 1998).

John Austin Baker, *The Faith of a Christian*, (London: Darton, Longman and Todd, 1996).

Marcus Braybrooke, *The Explorer's Guide to Christianity*, (London: Hodder and Stoughton, 1998)

Doctrine Commission of the Church of England, *We Believe in God*, (London: Church House Publishing, 1987).

Tom H. Driver, *Patterns of Grace*, (San Francisco: Harper and Row, 1977).

Tom H. Driver, *Christ in a Changing World*, (London: SCM Press, 1981).

Richard Giles, *We do not presume. ..*, (Norwich: Canterbury Press, 1998).

Brian Hebblethwaite, *The Essence of Christianity*, (London: SPCK, 1996).

Martin Henry, *On Not Understanding God*, (Dublin: The Columba Press, 1997).

Alister McGrath, *Understanding Doctrine. Its Purpose and Relevance for Today*, (London: Hodder and Stoughton, 1990).

Alister McGrath, *The Renewal of Anglicanism*, (London: SPCK, 1993).

Alister McGrath, *Christian Theology: An Introduction*, (Oxford: Blackwell Publishers Ltd, 1994).

Alister McGrath, *A Passion for Truth – the intellectual coherence of evangelicalism*, (Leicester: Apollos, 1996).

John Macquarrie, *The Principles of Christian Theology*, (London: SCM Press, 1966 & 1977).

John Macquarrie, *Christology Revisited*, (London: SCM Press, 1998).

Michael Mayne, *This Sunrise of Wonder*, (London: Fount/Harper Collins, 1995).

Hugh Montefiore, Ed., *The Gospel and Contemporary Culture*, (London: Mowbray, 1992).

Hugh Montefiore, *Credible Christianity: The Gospel in Contemporary Culture*, (London: Mowbray, 1993).

Lesslie Newbiggin, *Proper Confidence*, (London: SPCK, 1995).

George Pattison, *The End of Theology – and the Task of Thinking about God*, (London: SCM Press, 1998).

Stephen Platten, Ed., with Graham James and Andrew Chandler, *New Soundings*, (London: Darton, Longman and Todd, 1997).

John Polkinghorne, *Reason and Reality*, (London: SPCK, 1991).

Michael Ramsey, *The Anglican Spirit*, Ed. Dale Coleman, (London: SPCK, 1991).

Tom Smail, *The Forgotten Father*, (London: Hodder and Stoughton, 1980).

Stephen Sykes, *The Story of Atonement*, (London: Darton, Longman and Todd, 1997).

Alec Vidler, Ed., *Soundings: Essays Concerning Christian Understanding*, (Cambridge: CUPress, 1962).

Maurice Wiles, *The Remaking of Christian Doctrine*, (London: SCM Press, 1974).

Notes

INTRODUCTION

1. John Macquarrie, *Two Worlds Are Ours: An Introduction to Christian Mysticism*, (London: SCM Press, 2004), p 99.

2. P. D. James, *Time to be in Earnest: A Fragment of Autobiography*, (London: Faber & Faber, 1999), p 173.

3. Kenneth Kearon, 'Ethics, Communities and the Future', in *A Time to Build, Essays for Tomorrow's Church*, Ed. Stephen R. White, (Dublin: APCK, 1999), p77.

4. Stanley Hauerwas, *With the Grain of the Universe*, (London: SCM Press, 2002), p 10.

5. John Macquarrie, *Christology Revisited*, (London: SCM Press, 1998,) pp 48-60.

6. Richard Giles, *We do not presume ...*, (Norwich: Canterbury Press, 1998), p 40.

CHAPTER ONE

1. Marc Ouellet, 'The message of Balthasar's Theology to modern theology', in *Communion*, Summer 1996, pp 270-299, p 271.

2. John Macquarrie, *The Principles of Christian Theology*, (London: SCM Press, 1966 & 1977), p v.

3. John Austin Baker, *The Faith of a Christian*, (London: Darton, Longman & Todd, 1996), p 5.

4. Ibid p 11.

5. Martin Henry, *On Not Understanding God*, (Dublin: Columba Press, 1997), p 36

6. Maurice Wiles, 'Belief, Openness and Religious Commitment', in *Theology*, Vol CI, No 801, May / June 1998, pp 163-171, p 168.

7. Michael Ramsey, 'The Anglican Spirit', in *The Anglican Spirit*, Ed. Dale Coleman, (London: SPCK, 1991), pp 11-22, p 19.

8. Søren Kierkegaard, *Fear and Trembling and The Sickness Unto*

Death, Trs Walter Lowrie, (Princeton, NJ: Princeton University Press, 1941 & 1954), p 130.

CHAPTER TWO

1. Stephen R. White, *Don Cupitt and the Future of Christian Doctrine*, (London: SCM Press, 1994) pp 206-212.

2. William Marshall, *The Passion of Christ*, (Dublin: Columba Press & APCK, 1997), pp 91-113.

3. Stephen Sykes, *The Story of Atonement*, (London: Darton, Longman and Todd Ltd, 1997).

4. J. Denny Weaver, *The Nonviolent Atonement*, (Grand Rapids, Michigan & Cambridge: William B. Eerdmans Publishing Co, 2001).

CHAPTER THREE

1. John Burnaby, 'Christian Prayer', in *Soundings*, Ed. A. R. Vidler, (Cambridge: Cambridge University Press, 1962), pp 219-237, pp 236-7.

2. Alister McGrath, *Understanding Doctrine*, (London: Hodder and Stoughton Ltd, 1990, Second Edition, 1995) p 55.

3. Properly understood, C. S. Lewis' argument from the feeling of hunger to the existence of food is a good example of such an argument.

4. Michael Ramsey, *The Christian Priest Today*, (London: SPCK, 1972 & 1985) p 14.

5. C. S. Lewis, *The Lion, the Witch, and the Wardrobe*, (London: Geoffrey Bles, 1950; Collins Lions, 1980) p 75.

6. The Doctrine Commission of the Church of England, *We Believe in God*, (London: Church House Publishing, 1987), p 104.

7. Tom Smail, *The Forgotten Father*, (London: Hodder and Stoughton Ltd, 1980 & 1990) p 13.

8. Ibid p 16.

9. Doctrine Commission, p 108.

10. H.A. Williams, *Poverty, Chastity, Obedience*, (Mitchell Beazley, 1975), p 111, Quoted in Michael Mayne, *This Sunrise of Wonder*, (London: Fount Paperbacks, 1995), p 277.

11. Stephen R. White, *Authority and Anglicanism*, (London: SCM Press, 1996) p 123.

12. Alister McGrath, *Understanding Doctrine. Its Purpose and Relevance for Today*, (London: Hodder and Stoughton Ltd, 1990), p 175.

CHAPTER FOUR

1. Linda Woodhead, 'Life in the Spirit: Contemporary and Christian Understandings of the Human Person', in *New Soundings*, Ed. Stephen Platten, Graham James and Andrew Chandler, (London: Darton, Longman & Todd, 1997), pp 118-140, pp 134-5.

2. Alister McGrath, *Understanding Doctrine*, (London: Hodder & Stoughton, 1990 & 1995), p 55.

3. Tom F. Driver, *Patterns of Grace*, (San Francisco: Harper and Row, 1977), pp 167-8.

4. I am not sure whether Janet Martin Soskice has used this phrase in print, but she certainly used it in lectures and tutorials during her time as Ethics Tutor at Ripon College, Cuddesdon.

CHAPTER FIVE

1. Stephen R. White, *Don Cupitt and the Future of Christian Doctrine*, (London: SCM Press, 1994), p 66.

2. Martin Henry, *On Not Understanding God*, (Dublin: Columba Press, 1997), p 111.

3. *Soundings*, Ed. Alec Vidler, (Cambridge: Cambridge University Press, 1962), p 145.

4. Michael Adie, *Held Together*, (London: Darton, Longman and Todd, 1997), p 59.

CHAPTER SIX

1. Michael Mayne, *This Sunrise of Wonder*, (London: Harper Collins, Fount, 1995) p 244.

2. H. A. Williams, 'Theology and Self-Awareness', in *Soundings*, Ed. Alec Vidler, (Cambridge: CUP, 1962), pp 69-101, p 79.

3. Ibid p 80.

4. Don Cupitt, *The New Christian Ethics*, (London: SCM Press, 1988), p 5.

5. For a fuller treatment of this, see Stephen R. White, *The Right True End of Love: Sexuality and the Contemporary Church*, (Dublin: Columba Press, 2005).

6. Michael Vasey, *Strangers and Friends: A New Exploration of Homosexuality and the Bible*, (London: Hodder and Stoughton Ltd, 1995).

7. John Barry, 'Out of Lambeth', *Church of Ireland Gazette*, 21 August, 1998, p 11.

CHAPTER SEVEN

1. *Church of Ireland General Synod Reports*, 1999, Report of the Standing Committee Sub-Committee on Sectarianism, pp 168-200, p 176.

2. Maurice Wiles, 'Belief, Openness and Religious Commitment', in *Theology*, Vol CI, No 801, May/June 1998. pp 163-171, pp 163-4.

3. Ibid p 171.

4. Ibid pp 168-9.

5. Stephen Sykes, *The Story of Atonement*, (London: Darton, Longman & Todd, 1997) p x.

6. *The Truth Shall Make You Free: The Lambeth Conference 1988*, (London: ACC, 1988), p 128.

CONCLUSION

1. Alister McGrath, *Understanding Doctrine, Its Purpose and Relevance for Today*, (London: Hodder and Stoughton Ltd, 1990), p 177.

2. Alister McGrath, *The Renewal of Anglicanism*, (London: SPCK, 1993), p 70.

3. A. R. Vidler, Appended note on 'Authority' and 'Liberty' in the Church, appended to, J. N. Sanders, 'The Meaning and Authority of the New Testament', in *Soundings*, Ed. A. R. Vidler, (Cambridge: CUPress, 1962), pp 123-145, p 145.

4. Marcus Braybrooke, *The Explorer's Guide to Christianity*,

(London: Hodder and Stoughton Ltd, 1998), p 10.

5. Ibid.

6. Ibid p 116.

7. Tom F. Driver, *Christ in a Changing World*, (London: SCM Press Ltd, 1981), pp 10-11.

Index of Names